Mary Pinińska was born in England of a Polish father and British mother but she moved back to Poland some years ago and now lives in Warsaw. Her other books include *A Little Polish Cookbook*, an illustrated *History of the Hotel Bristol*, the award winning *Another Landscape Revealed* written with Poland's premier chef, Bernard Lussiana, and *Poland's Gourmet Cuisine*.

The
Polish
Kitchen

Mary Pinińska

GRUB STREET · LONDON

To Alex,
with love and thanks for sharing my table
— all over the world.

Published by
Grub Street
4 Rainham Close
London SW11 6SS

Reprinted 2007
Reprinted 2008

Copyright this revised edition © Grub Street 2000
Text Copyright © Mary Pinińska 2000
Cover illustration by Kate Miller
First published in 1990 by Macmillan London Limited

The moral right of the author has been asserted.

British Library Cataloguing in Publication Data
Pinińska, Mary
    The Polish Kitchen
    1. Cookery, Polish 2. Food habits – Poland
    I. Title
    641.5'9438

ISBN-13: 978-1-902304-56-4

Typeset by Pearl Graphics, Hemel Hempstead
Printed and bound in India by Replika Press Pvt. Ltd.

. . . At his sign
the servants entered two by two in line,
and brought the dishes round: the soup of beet,
called Royal, and Polish broth prepared from meat
in which the Seneschal to all unknown
a piece of money and some pearls had thrown
it purifies the blood and guards the health.
Then other dishes – who could tell their wealth!
and who today would understand their names,
those famous dishes *kontuz, arkas, blemas**
with cod and stuffing, musk and caramel,
pine nuts and civet, damson plums as well.
Those fish! dry salmon from the Danube far,
and Turkish and Venetian caviare,
a pike and pickerel both large and small,
flounders, and fat and noble carp and all.
The last of all, a rare and secret dish,
consisted of a single uncut fish,
fried at the head and roasted in the mid,
its tail in a ragout with sauces hid.

*kontuz = a sort of sausage
arkas = a cold dish of milk, cream and yolks of eggs
blemas = almond jelly

An extract from 'The Last Feast' in *Pan Tadeusz*
by Adam Mickiewicz (1798-1855)
translated by Kenneth MacKenzie (1964).

CONTENTS

ACKNOWLEDGEMENTS

I owe thanks to many people for their help in compiling this book: to Princess Lew Sapieha for her encouragement at the beginning of this project; to Mrs Płodowska for generously sharing many of her recipes with me; and to Dr Andrzej Rottermund for providing me with transcripts of the relevant chapters in Fr. Jędrzej Kitowiez's *The Descriptions of Customs Under the Rule of Augustus III* and also a selection of Paweł Trerno's recipes from the collection in the Jagiellonian University in Cracow.

I am grateful to the following for giving me recipes for this book: Andrzej Badziak; Mrs Cielecka; Dorota Cywińska, who lent me several old and very interesting family cook books; Marzena Czubowicz; Zosia Davidson, who also spared time to translate some recipes for me; Mrs Gawlikowska; Mrs Gumińska; the Jabłonowski family; Dorota Komornicka; Stefan Komornicki; Juliusz Komornicki; Mrs Łepkowska; Teresa Mirgos; John Pomian; P.M. Przypkowski, who kindly sent me extracts from some of the eighteenth and nineteenth century cookery books in his museum in Jędrzejów, Poland; Countess Ronikier; Princess Lew Sapieha; Mrs Szymaniak; Ania Walles; Wierzyriek's Restaurant in Cracow, who supplied me with recipes for five of their best dishes; and Count Jerzy Wolański who sought out some excellent old cookery books for me.

I would like to acknowledge two cookery books from which I have extracted recipes: *Cooking the Polish Way* by Lili Kowalska (Paul Hamlyn, 1964) whose recipes are on pages 46, 62, 76, 100, 132, 133 and 147; and *Continental European Cooking* by Maria Disslowa (Tern [Rybitwa] Book Co. Ltd, 1952) whose recipes appear on pages 21, 24, 90, 115 and 117.

I would like to thank the late Juliusz Komornicki and his wife Anna, with whom I stayed during my visit to Poland while working on this book. They gave me every possible help, and Uncle Julek was a tireless and meticulous translator . I thank Janet Williams, who came to look after my son – born in the middle of this – at critical moments in the progress of the manuscript, and did so with unsurpassed skill and devotion.

Lastly, but most importantly I would like to express my gratitude to my father, Jan Badeni, for embuing me with not only with an interest in food but also in the customs and culinary traditions of the country he came from.

INTRODUCTION TO POLISH FOOD

The shape and form of a nation's cuisine is at first wholly dependent on its soil and climate. In later years it may also be moulded and polished by its proximity to trading routes, and by wars, foreign influences, economic prosperity, religion and so on, but its basic characteristics remain. The elementary ingredients of Poland's cuisine were dictated by the rich, dark soil and the harsh northern climate, which yielded cereal crops such as rye, wheat, millet, barley and buckwheat. From these came bread: from rye the beautifully dark, dense, moist loaves so typical of this part of Europe; and, from other grains, white bread with which soups were made and whose stale crumbs were used to thicken and bind stuffings and sauces. Fried breadcrumbs have long been used as a garnish in Polish cooking, and *à la Polonaise*, which means a garnish of fried breadcrumbs, often with diced hardboiled egg, is part of international gastronomic vocabulary. Bread has always had enormous symbolic importance to Poles, and for many years has been subsidised by the state. As well as state run bread shops, there are numerous private bakeries, and these can be traced both by their tempting aroma of fresh bread and by the inevitable queue stretching out along the street.

Cereals remain widely used in the Polish kitchen, not only for bread but also for the ancient dessert stews sweetened with honey which are still eaten (but mainly just at Christmas, in the form of *kutia*, a whole-wheat stew). It is buckwheat, however, which is most often seen today. Considered the finest of all the cereals, buckwheat is Poland's most popular side dish, and, in varying forms such as fried or baked, frequently accompanies meat or game dishes.

Vegetables were also grown, but only those that could be stored, pickled or preserved to last through the long cold winters. Pickled cabbage (sauerkraut), pickled cucumbers, mushrooms, beetroot preserved in vinegar, kohlrabi and many root vegetables became entwined with other elements of the national cuisine, and remain a quintessential part of Polish cooking. Sauerkraut, much used as a vegetable and as a filling for *pierogi*, the Polish ravioli, among other things, is sold at market and grocery shops by the ladleful, fresh from large wooden barrels. It can also be easily bought in bottles under the Krakus label both in England and Poland, as can pickled beetroot and cucumber. Other vegetables form part of the main meal: kohlrabi, for example, is often stuffed with meat and baked.

Soups were made from all these vegetables and this book contains traditional Polish recipes for sauerkraut soup, sour cucumber soup, beetroot, mushroom and kohlrabi soup. Many of these originated in ancient times and have travelled into the twentieth century with little or no alteration. An enormous variety of mushrooms are dried as well as pickled, and in this form they are used to flavour soups, stocks and sauces. Popular from earliest times, mushrooms really came into their own during the tenth century when Catholicism was accepted into Poland, and following the Catholic rite meant that strict fasting was observed on holy days and Fridays, neither meat nor animal fats being eaten on such occasions. Soups were based on vegetable stocks and fermented grain, while oil made from poppy seeds, almonds, hemp and flax replaced butter. Mushrooms became a substitute for meat – as did fish – and many dishes grew from this, such as mushroom cutlets, mushroom and rice-filled cabbage leaves, and mushrooms in sour cream. Today, dried Polish mushrooms are exported all over the world and at home remain a pillar of the kitchen.

In the sixteenth, seventeenth and eighteenth centuries variety was introduced to this main core of vegetables in the form of salad ingredients, green vegetables and potatoes. When the Italian Princess Bona Sforza went to Poland in 1518 to marry King Zygmunt the Old, her retinue, disdainful of the Poles' love of meat, promoted green salads and many green vegetables. A number of foods which were presumably introduced at this time, such as tomatoes, chicory, asparagus, artichokes and onions, as well as salad itself, have Polish names which are extremely similar to the Italian. In some cases Polish names for vegetables are described as Italian: for example, savoy cabbage is *kapusta włoska* which means 'Italian cabbage', and the vegetables used to flavour a stock – onions, carrots and parsley – and the most basic of green vegetables are known as *Włoszczyzna* which translates as 'things Italian'.

Potatoes first arrived in Poland in the seventeenth century, via Vienna, where King Jan Sobieski had, after the Battle of Vienna, seen them at the Emperor's residence and asked for some tubers to be sent to Wilanów, his summer palace outside Warsaw. They only became known among the aristocracy, however, and it was not until the late eighteenth century that they achieved popularity throughout the rest of the country, when they were introduced by the Germans who settled on Royal estates in Poland at about this time.

Meat was of great significance in the Polish diet and remains so today, despite attempts by the Italians in the sixteenth century to persuade the Poles to reduce their meat intake. It is ironic that in a country where meat is hard to come by and extremely expensive the population should regard it as an everyday necessity. This always seems to have been the case, in all strata of society, although of course the cut and quality of the meat would vary according to the housekeeper's purse. Chicken, pork, beef and game have long been the most popular meats. Pork has always been used in large quantities to make *kiełbasa*, the Polish sausage, and for the tasty hams which are widely eaten. These items would be the pride of the peasant's table, and the pig would be fattened up with them in mind. Nowadays, *kiełbasas* and hams are exported worldwide, but in Poland the variety of pork products, smoked, cooked or both make a tempting and impressive display in the shops.

Game has always flourished in Poland, in the many forests scattered over the countryside which make ideal breeding grounds. For the peasants living in or near the forests and for the middle and upper classes in nearby towns, game was the staple diet. Big game such as wild boar is even more prolific today than it was in the past, but is still hard to find in meat shops, primarily because of the cost. In restaurants, however, it is fairly well represented, with more than one or two classic wild boar recipes usually on offer. Partridges, pheasants and other small game birds are a little easier to buy but, like all game, are extremely expensive, being considered the choicest of meats.

The idea of pickling and preserving was not limited to vegetables: herring, fished in the Baltic, was soused with spices and vinegar and in this form could be transported across the country to places which would not otherwise get sea-fish. It would also keep extremely well in the larder to be used, among other things, for fast days and holy days. This method of treating herring has remained popular throughout the Baltic countries, and in Poland is a favourite national food.

Again with the accent on storage, sour cream, curd cheese and soured milk became important constituents of the Polish kitchen. Fresh cream and milk would be left to ferment, and would keep for some time in their 'sour' form. Curd cheese, made from the separated curds of cow's milk, keeps in its unripe state for a considerable time and was popular for cheesecakes, as a filling for pancakes or in little savoury patties. it has a delicious, slightly acid flavour and is eaten quite often in Poland on bread with a sprinkling of salt. Despite the advent of refrigeration, these dairy products are still an essential element in the taste and flavour of Polish cooking. Sour cream is added to soups, mixed with flour to thicken sauces, poured on salads as a dressing or simply used as a decoration on certain dishes. It is enormously popular, and can be bought in any food shop with a choice between 12%, 18% or 22% fat.

Honey was used to sweeten food and drink, and bee-keeping became all important industry. *Kutia*, a wholewheat stew, is one of several dishes sweetened with honey which are still made and which date from early times.

For seasoning, salt and spices were used. Salt was an expensive commodity, but one indigenous to Poland. The salt mines outside Cracow, Wieliczka, began to be mined intensively in the thirteenth century, and before long their value to Poland was such that a protective town wall with many towers and a royal castle was built around them. Open to tourists since the 1930s, these mines are well worth a visit. They contain hall after underground hall of superb salt sculptures, including chapels containing saints, altars and pulpits, as well as salt gnomes, stalactites and lake caverns. Perhaps most remarkable of all is the sparkling, shimmering chapel of St Kinga, which was excavated in the seventeenth century and made into a shrine during the nineteenth and early twentieth centuries by the Markowski brothers. This chapel, with the dimensions of a ballroom, is lit by five ornate salt chandeliers.

Poland's position on the great European trading routes meant that spices were introduced early to the Polish table. Different cities of course had varying influences. Lwów, for example, one of the great cities of the South, was a cosmopolitan mix of Poles, Ruthenians, Moldavians, Jews, Germans and Armenians and had frequently to fend off attacks by invading Tartars and Turks. It is thought that the Turkish trading route was responsible for the introduction of many of the sweet spices such as cloves, as well as for raisins and figs, almonds and rosewater, and perhaps even for the now typically Polish *mazurek*, the flat pastry cake topped with a variety of nuts and fruits under an egg or sugar glaze. Imported spices were beyond the purse of the ordinary cook, who had to rely on Polish seasonings such as juniper berries, mushrooms, salt and sour cream.

As well as religion, foreign traders, the Italians and later the French, Polish cuisine was influenced by the large Jewish population which sought refuge in the country during the fourteenth century, as it was one of the few places in Europe which at that time practised religious tolerance. They brought with them many traditional Jewish dishes which have been incorporated into Polish cooking, the most well known of which is pike or carp cooked the Jewish way (see page 187).

At its height the great Polish-Lithuanian Commonwealth stretched from the Marches of Brandenburg in the west to beyond Smolensk and Kursk in the east, and from the Baltic in the north to the Black Sea in the south. This enormous country was larger than any other in Europe, and embraced much of what is today considered European Russia. Because many of the same crops were grown throughout this vast fertile area, Polish and Russian food has much in common, including the frequent use of cereals, beetroot and cabbage, and the making of sour cream, pancakes and *pierogi*. However, while Russian cooking remained relatively unchanged, Polish food was subject to the refining influences of Italian and subsequently French cuisine, as representatives of these nations married Polish monarchs, bringing with them their national culinary habits and ideas. An example of this is the omelette, which arrived in Poland during the late seventeeth century, via the French wife of King Jan Sobieski III.

Father Jędrzej Kitowicz, writing in the 1780s, gives us an idea, in *The Descriptions of Customs Under the Rule of Augustus III*, his fascinating history of food and manners, of the changes brought about by these foreign influences. He states that at the time of Augustus III (1733-63), popular dishes were *barszcz*, broth, boiled beef, goose with cream and dried mushrooms served with pearl barley, and black goose – the recipe for which was as follows:

First the cook had to burn some straw (if he could not find any he took some out of his boots) then he added one tablespoon of raw honey, some strong vinegar, pepper and ginger and when mixed this would make the bird black.

Other dishes were tripe cooked with saffron, white veal with cream, lamb with garlic, sausages, venison and game. Spices and other flavourings used were almonds, raisins, nutmeg, pepper, saffron, pistachio nuts, cloves, ginger, pine kernels, mushrooms, honey, sugar, rice and occasionally lemons. As lemons were very expensive they were used little, vinegar being the more usual alternative, but all these ingredients would have only been seen in the houses of rich burghers, wealthy land-owners and the aristocracy. The peasantry and urban poor – in fact the majority of the population – were unable to afford imported goods and still relied on produce from the countryside. Vegetables eaten at that time by all strata of society were carrots, parsnips, turnips, beetroot and cabbage.

In 1764, however, when Stanisław Augustus Poniatowski, the last King of Poland, came to the throne, the influence of French cuisine began to be felt. His chef, Paweł Tremo, created some wonderful dishes (such as the Pike with Natural Sauce on page 42), combining the virtues of French cooking with the old traditions of the Polish kitchen. Tremo was renowned as a superb chef, and a collection of his recipes, although not in print today, has been preserved in the library of the Jagiellonian University in Cracow. (Obviously he also had a sense of humour, as on the title page there is a motto 'Not everybody thinks but everybody eats.')

Because of this French influence, black goose fell from favour, and was served only at funerals and in the provinces. Even then it was cooked with sugar, cloves and lemon rather than vinegar. Lemons became cheaper and were used extensively. Pistachio nuts and pine kernels were replaced by capers, olives anchovies, truffles and oysters. Wine was used in cooking, especially in fish dishes. Cakes and pastries improved considerably, and Kitowizi praises the doughnut, which he says could 'be blown off a plate by the wind' whereas before you 'risked having your eye blackened by one'.

This French influence on Polish cuisine, however, only really affected the rich and aristocratic: the rest of the nation still relied on Polish favourites. Staple soups such as *krupnik* (barley soup), *kapuśniak* (cabbage soup) and *grochówka* (yellow pea soup) graced their tables, with the better off adding *zrazy* (beef), tripe or some form of sausage to the meal. These dishes are typical of those that are still eaten today.

The development of Polish cuisine was halted, even reversed, by the outbreak of the Second World War. As in any country at war, rationing was introduced and food was scarce, but after the war the situation improved little. Poland's natural resources, such as coal, were given at a loss to the Soviet Union in the ten years or so immediately after the war, when they could have been bringing in much-needed hard currency. Food was no longer imported, and the Polish countryside which now had to feed the entire country was struggling to return to normal after the devastations of the war. With the subsequent arrangement whereby the state fixed the prices for which farmers sold their produce, there was little or no incentive to produce more. Rationing was lifted only briefly and reintroduced in the 1970s, when large amounts of Polish food were being exported in order to bring in foreign money. It remained on various goods, such as meat, until August 1989, when price rises and the empty shops caused by its abolition led to hardship on a scale unmatched since the last war – half a century after its outbreak.

The food found in the Polish home today is remarkably traditional. Although a decade and more of freedom which has allowed Poles to travel more easily has made its mark with foreign food becoming more and more common among the younger generation. Whereas once the idea of choosing a recipe and going out to buy the required ingredients was impossible, now all that you could expect to find in a capital city is there to buy. The countryside still has a long way to catch up with Warsaw and the bigger towns but the population there is far less demanding and of course the many foreign supermarket chains are far less present. The hardships that existed for so long however, meant that the sophisticated trappings and trimmings of foreign influences which Polish cooking had acquired before the Second World War, were lost and the cuisine returned to the elements upon which it was founded, as only ingredients for the most basic dishes were to be found and even those often involved a long queue. Cakes and pastries were less affected by the food shortages, despite butter and sugar being rationed for many years and eggs scarce and exorbitant (one egg from a private stall was equivalent to £12.00 sterling).

Despite the difficulties and hardships surrounding food in Poland, it has always remained central to people's lives. Hospitality is part of the national character and in any Polish home, food, however meagre, will always be shared warmly with a guest or passer-by. This is reflected in the Christmas and Easter custom in which blessed water and hardboiled eggs are shared between all those present. Catholicism still influences the national diet, and the Christmas feast remains a meatless one, with fasting adhered to on certain other holy days. In the normal course of events the main meal of the day is lunch, which is eaten between 1 and 4 p.m. and normally consists of three courses, such as soup and a meat dish followed by a cake or pastry. Supper at around 6 to 8 p.m. is lighter – Polish sausage, bread, salami, herring in sour cream, and a cucumber salad followed by a poppy-seed roll or other sweet cakes is a fairly standard example of what might be eaten. Both these meals will probably – depending on the individual – be preceded by vodka, and vodka or wine will accompany the food as well. As the working day runs from approximately 8 a.m. until 3.30 or 4 p.m., breakfast is early. Breakfasts are delicious, and include hunks of fresh rye bread, slices of hard-boiled egg, salamis, white cheese, toast, jam and coffee.

Polish eating tends to happen at home, but this habit is changing due to the plethora of new restaurants which have sprung up. Not only that, but as more and more Western countries have businesses in Poland they have influenced the working hours, eating habits and financial possibilities of their Polish staff. Therefore the young successful Polish businessman is now as likely to entertain in a restaurant as his counterpart in another European country. Some things remain sacred however, such as celebrations or family get-togethers where it would be seen as inappropriate to do anything except entertain at home. Friends and relations are normally invited to nameday's (the Saint's day after whom people are named and celebrated in preference to birthdays) at which food, wine and dancing will be in good supply. The guest's contribution on these occasions is normally a floral one. The giving of flowers is a strong tradition in Poland and what makes it all the more valued is that flowers are particularly expensive. The care with which they are wrapped, in the little flower kiosks on street corners, is exquisite, and the flower seller will decorate the flowers with greenery before encasing them in cellophane and adding ribbons and bows.

It is impossible to overstate the changes which have occurred in all aspects of Polish life since the beginning of the 1990's. However, the culture of the Polish table has remained comfortingly familiar. While so many countries have thrown off their culinary traditions in honour of convenience, sophistication or lack of national pride, Poland has made no such move. Foreign food is treated with interest and even enthusiasm, but it has its place, and it is not at the family table for the religious feasts of Christmas or Easter where from mother to daughter the same Polish dishes are as lovingly prepared as they were in the times of war and hardship which we hope will never return.

The Polish eating habits are though gradually changing to a healthier pattern. Wine, once so hard to find in palatable form, is now drunk more often at dinners than vodka. Increasingly, oil is used to cook in instead of pork fat. Fish, once relegated to being merely a religious substitute for meat, is becoming easier to buy and more and more popular.

Polish food has much to offer and the Pole's love of food is a pleasure to share. The well-known hospitality in Poland and the pride with which any foreigner is served with a Polish dish are characteristics which I am sure will always exist. In the modern invasion of foreign influences through recipes, restaurants and the dreaded fast food, I believe that the culture of the Polish table, its way of cooking and its use of ingredients will remain as steadfast as it has done through other more threatening attempts to weaken its identity. I hope that those who read this book will find among its pages many reasons to rejoice that the Polish kitchen is still alive and strong . . .

SOUPS

Soups have been drunk in Poland since earliest times. They were served not only at lunch and dinner as they are today, but also at breakfast, until the introduction of coffee in the late seventeenth century. (Coffee slowly made its way into Polish homes after their victory over the Turks at the Battle of Vienna in 1683, which resulted in large quantities of Turkish coffee being taken as booty.) The earliest breakfast soups were made from beer, into which egg yolks were beaten when the soup was boiling, and a little sour cream or sugar was stirred in for flavour. Slightly later, and more favoured by the ladies, wine soups were drunk (rather similar to mulled wine), and these were flavoured with cinnamon, sugar, cloves and sweet cream. When coffee and eventually tea replaced soups as breakfast beverages it, not surprisingly, helped to reduce the alcohol problem in the country.

At lunch and dinner, though, the rich diversity of Polish soups meant that they were drunk throughout the year. Ancient in origin and particularly Polish, untouched by foreign sophistication, are yellow-pea soup, sauerkraut soup, barley soup, sour-rye soup, mushroom soup and potato soup, which reflect the ingredients available on the land. Chunks of sausage, bacon, slices of egg, croûtons, grains, mushrooms and other vegetables can all be found in these soups, and a simple method of cooking prevailed, with ingredients being slowly stewed in stock or water until tender. To thicken soups such as these a little flour was beaten in, or alternatively chopped pork fat (*słonina*) was fried and mixed with flour and a little water and then added to the soup. A characteristic flavouring was sour milk or sour cream of which there would always have been a ready supply in the country kitchen.

Although these soups were enjoyed by the burghers, nobles and aristocracy who could, unlike the peasantry, afford the luxury of imported goods and whose chefs were influenced by culinary ideas from abroad, they retained their rustic quality and still provide today the simple wholesome goodness, warmth and nourishment necessary during the chill winter months.

Although these soups were, as mentioned above, drunk by the middle and upper classes *en famille*, they would rarely have been given to their guests, except at, for instance, winter shooting parties where the inner glow guaranteed by sauerkraut or barley soup suited the occasion perfectly. For guests at the dinner table, chefs would prepare a delicate crayfish soup or one of the more elegant clear soups such as *barszcz* (pages 164 and 184) – the well-known clear beetroot soup, also ancient in origin, with recipes dating back to the fourteenth century – or rosół, a clear meat stock. A pastry garnish or little dumplings of some sort would normally accompany the clear soups, and garnishes remain a typical feature of Polish cooking. Choux-paste peas bob on a thin pea soup, while French noodles or egg drops decorate a consommé. 'Little Ears', so called because of their shape, are the tiny dumplings traditionally served with *barszcz*. These are filled with meat or, for holy days and fast days when meat is forbidden, with mushrooms.

Also typical of Polish soups was the balance of sweet and sour. By the use of fermented juice, tart fruits or pickled vegetables, a soup would be given a sharpness strong enough to flavour it without destroying or overpowering the other elements of the dish. Sweetness would be achieved by the addition of a little sugar or sweet cream.

In summer, cold soups were drunk, varying in content according to region. In the north-west of Poland, fruit soups were popular, perhaps in part due to German influence, whereas in the east of the country, iced vegetable soups such as cucumber or the Lithuanian dish *chłodnik* (cold beetroot soup) were more common.

The only difference between earlier recipes and those of today is that any regional variations have all but disappeared. Apart from the natural tendency for this to happen anyway, in the twentieth century, this is mainly due to the changing borders of the country after the Second World War and the subsequent relocation of so many people to different parts of the country. I am sure, however, that many people fondly remember dishes from their childhood, and it is for this reason that traditions and customs will never be totally lost.

YELLOW-PEA SOUP
Grochówka

Legend relates that in olden days when a young man was known to be coming to ask for the hand of a daughter of the house, he would always be served yellow-pea soup with little pigtails in it. If the pigtails were lying in the soup it meant rejection, but if they were standing upright it signified consent. If the wooer was served the 'refusal' version, he normally left straight after that course. Brokenhearted he might have departed, but not hungry: this is a thick, filling and warming soup, and the traditional Polish ingredients make it a meal on its own. Yellow-pea soup is very popular in Poland and is now served – as far as I know – with no ulterior motives!

Serves 2

....

(1 tablespoon yellow split peas per person;
   ¹/₂ tablespoon barley per person)
2 tablespoons yellow split peas
1 tablespoon pearl barley
4 rashers smoked bacon, diced
salt and pepper
1 clove garlic, crushed
pinch dried marjoram

....

Soak the peas and barley overnight in cold water to cover. The next day drain peas and barley, cover with fresh water, add the bacon to this and season. Bring to the boil and simmer for 45-60 minutes, until the soup is thick and the peas are soft; the barley will not disintegrate. Season again and add the garlic and marjoram just before serving.

SOUP OF GOOSE GIBLETS WITH LIVER DUMPLINGS
Zupa z Gęsich Podróbek z Pulpetami

Goose giblets can only be bought by buying the goose itself, so this soup is ideal for left-over giblets after Christmas. The rich and tasty broth is enhanced by the addition of these very Polish dumplings.

Serves 8

For the stock:
2 carrots
1 celery stick
1 leek
1 onion
1 bunch parsley
1.5 litres (2¹/₂ pints) water
salt and pepper

giblets from 2 geese
50 g (2 oz) pearl barley
4-5 dried mushrooms, washed and soaked
25 g (1 oz) butter
300 ml (¹/₂ pint) single cream

For the dumplings:
75 g (3 oz) white dried breadcrumbs
25 g (1 oz) butter
1 egg yolk
1 egg
plain flour for dusting

Prepare a stock by putting the carrots, celery stick, leek, onion and parsley into cold water. Season. Bring to the boil and simmer for 30 minutes.

Remove the livers from the goose giblets and put to one side. Put all the remaining giblets into the stock and simmer gently for 1¹/₂ hours. In a separate pan, cover the pearl barley with cold water, add the mushrooms and simmer for 1-1¹/₂ hours. When the pearl barley is tender but not disintegrated, mix the butter into the cream and pour it into the broth.

To make the dumplings, chop the livers very finely and mix them with the breadcrumbs, butter, egg yolk and egg. Knead it for a minute or so to form a dough, then pull pieces off it and form small balls. Lightly flour a wooden board, roll the balls in the flour and drop them into the soup. Leave to simmer for 20 minutes. Pour into a tureen and serve.

Sauerkraut Soup
Kapuśniak

This is a typical Polish winter soup — nourishing, filling and very simple to make. It is often drunk at shoots, which can take place at temperatures of −20°C, and sauerkraut or barley soup, vodka and Hunter's Stew (see page 165) are the forces used to combat the cold.

In Poland sauerkraut is sold from wooden barrels by the ladleful, and purchasers bring with them suitable containers into which it is transferred. In Britain it is widely available in jars of various sizes from most supermarkets. It varies in sourness according to the make or batch, and should always be rinsed once before use, rinsing again to decrease the sourness if necessary. The addition of lemon juice increases the sourness if it is too sweet. It does not need to be cooked when bought in this form, but may be warmed through for a softer texture.

Serves 4

25 g (1 oz) butter
4 spare ribs
200 g (7 oz) sauerkraut
1 onion, peeled and sliced
1 bay leaf
2 dried mushrooms, soaked overnight
1.25 litres (2 pints) water

Heat the butter in a small frying pan and fry the spare ribs briskly to seal in their juices. Gently boil the ribs and all the other ingredients in the water for about 10 minutes, stirring occasionally, until the sauerkraut softens. Remove the spare ribs and bay leaf, season to taste and serve.

BARLEY SOUP
Krupnik

This is another traditional, warming Polish Soup, and one often served in freezing temperatures at shooting parties in winter.

Serves 4

....

4 spare ribs
3 dried mushrooms, washed and soaked
3 tablespoons pinhead barley
quarter of an onion, finely chopped
1 litre (1³/₄ pints) cold water
milk or sour cream
salt and pepper
1 teaspoon chopped parsley

....

Put the spare ribs, mushrooms, barley and onion in a large pan and cover with the water. Simmer for about an hour until the barley is really soft, continuing to add water when necessary. Thin it with a little milk or sour cream. Remove the bones, season, add the chopped parsley and serve.

POTATO SOUP
Kartoflanka

Potatoes have never outranked cereals in popularity in Poland, but they are eaten widely and frequently served cut into thick slices and added to soups, as in this recipe.

Serves 4

....

1.5 litres (2½ pints) water
1 beef stock cube
1 carrot, sliced
1 onion, peeled and sliced
1 tablespoon parsley
2 large potatoes, peeled and sliced
1 heaped tablespoon plain flour
4 slices unsmoked streaky bacon, rind removed
250 ml (scant ½ pint) water
salt and pepper

....

Bring the water to the boil and dissolve the stock cube in it. Add the carrot, onion, parsley and potatoes and simmer until the potatoes are soft. Chop the bacon and fry it in a small frying pan. When it is cooked add it to the soup. Sprinkle the flour over the remaining bacon fat, mix well and cook gently until golden. Remove from the heat and add 250 ml cold water. Mix until smooth, and add to the soup. Season, bring to the boil and serve.

ONION SOUP
Zupa Cebulowa

There is a story that in 1668, when King Jan Kazimierz was leaving Poland for France after abdicating his throne, he stopped before crossing the border in order to have one last taste of Polish Onion Soup.

Serves 6

300 g (10^1/$_2$ oz) onions
50 g (2 oz) butter
4 slices brown bread
2 litres (3^1/$_2$ pints) lean beef stock
5 cloves
^{1}/$_2$ clove nutmeg, finely grated
^{1}/$_4$ teaspoon ground ginger
salt

Dice the onions and fry them in half the butter until golden. With the remaining butter, fry the whole slices of bread until they are coloured. In a large saucepan, heat the stock and add the onions, bread and cloves to it. Simmer for ten minutes, and then force the mixture through a sieve. Reheat the soup and add the nutmeg, ginger and salt to taste.

SOUR CUCUMBER SOUP
Zupa Ogórkowa

This recipe was generously given to me by Kuba Plodowska, whose knowledge of Polish cooking is extensive, and I am very grateful to her for sharing many of her recipes and culinary ideas with me. (Kuba's ancestors, members of one of the richer noble families, the Cielecki, fought at the Battle of Vienna in 1683, under King Jan Sobieski III who saved Europe from the Turks. The Cielecki armorials, *Zaremba*, still adorn the chapel at Kahlenburg high above the Austrian capital.)

Serves 4

....

1 litre (1³/₄ pints) chicken stock
2 medium-sized potatoes
2 medium-sized cucumbers pickled in brine
25 g (1 oz) butter
150 ml (¹/₄ pint) sour cream
1 teaspoon plain flour
salt and pepper

....

Heat the stock. Peel and dice the potatoes and boil them in the stock until soft. Peel the cucumbers and grate them coarsely. Melt the butter over a gentle heat and soften the grated cucumber in it. Add to the stock and potatoes. Taste and add a little brine if necessary – the soup should have a pleasantly sour taste. Mix the sour cream with the flour and stir in a spoonful of hot soup. Return this mixture to the soup and season. Serve immediately, without bringing back to the boil.

KOHLRABI SOUP
Zupa z Kalarepy

Kohlrabi is one of the more common Polish vegetables. It matures quickly, withstands frost and can be stored for some time, all of which make it an ideal ingredient of the Polish kitchen. Its flavour is similar to the turnip's, but more delicate, and its slightly nutty taste comes out beautifully in this soup.

Serves 4

....

          400 g (14 oz) kohlrabi
          1 onion
          2 carrots
          $^1/_2$ teaspoon fresh parsley, chopped
          500 ml (scant 1 pint) water
          500 ml (scant 1 pint) milk
          cooked noodles – you can either use 2 tablespoons
               of dried short-cut macaroni noodles or follow the
               recipe for Egg Drops on page 25
          salt and pepper

....

Peel and slice the kohlrabi and cook with the other vegetables and the parsley in the water. When the vegetables are soft, liquidise the soup and stir in the milk. Reheat, stir in the cooked noodles or follow the recipe for egg drops, season to taste and serve.

POLISH SOUR RYE SOUP
Żurek Polski

This is a recipe from Wierzynek's, a famous restaurant housed in a beautiful ancient building behind a classical facade just off the magnificent market square in Cracow. It is basically a vegetable soup flavoured with *kwas* (literally, 'acid'), the name given to the fermented juice (see below) which is used to sour soups. Beetroot can be added to *kwas* at the outset of its fermentation thus making sour beet juice, and this is the basis for the well-known Polish soup *barszcz* (see pages 164 and 184). You will need to make the *kwas* four or five days before you make the soup.

Serves 6

For the kwas:
75 g (2¹/₂ oz) wholemeal rye flour*
600 ml (1 pint) boiled, cooled water
¹/₄ clove garlic

For the soup:
1.25 litres (2 pints) stock from vegetables and beef bones
100 g (3¹/₂ oz) bacon
100 g (3¹/₂ oz) onion
1 tablespoon dried mushrooms, washed and soaked in
    warm water for 30 minutes
400 ml (³/₄ pint) kwas
300 ml (¹/₂ pint) single cream
salt and pepper
¹/₄ teaspoon marjoram
¹/₂ clove garlic, crushed

To serve:
eggs, hard-boiled
smoked sausage
potatoes, cooked and diced

To make the *kwas*, rinse out an earthenware jar or any other non-aluminium vessel with boiling water (aluminium would react with the acidity of the *kwas*). Put the flour in the jar and mix to a liquid paste with a little of the water. Leave the mixture to settle for a few minutes, and then pour on the remaining boiled water. Chop the garlic and add. Cover the top of the jar with muslin or pierced cling film and leave in a warm place for 4 or 5 days to ferment. Strain and use as required. If stored in an airtight container, it will keep for some weeks.

To make the soup, heat the stock, chop the bacon and onion and add these to it. Simmer for 10 minutes. In a separate pan, gently cook the mushrooms in the soaking water until soft. Chop them finely and add them and their water to the stock. Add the *kwas* and the cream, and season with salt, pepper, marjoram and garlic.

Serve with hard-boiled eggs, fried smoked sausage and diced cooked potatoes.

*A crust of rye bread, available from most bakeries or supermarkets, can be substituted for the flour if necessary. The whole crust should be placed in the jar with the other ingredients and left to ferment as above.

DILL SOUP
Zupa Koperkowa

Dill is *the* Polish flavouring. It is mixed with sour cream for salad dressings, tossed with boiled potatoes, sprinkled on fish and used for sauces, to name but a few uses. Here are two versions of dill soup.

DILL SOUP I

Serves 2

....

15 g (¹/₂ oz) unsalted butter
1 heaped tablespoon fresh dill, chopped
500 ml (scant 1 pint) beef stock
¹/₂ teaspoon lemon juice
150 ml (¹/₄ pint) single cream
salt and pepper

....

Melt the butter in a pan, add the dill and stir gently over a low heat for a few minutes. Heat the stock and add the dill to it. Mix in the lemon juice and cream. Season and serve.

DILL SOUP II

This is a slightly thicker soup than Version I.

Serves 2-3

....

1 litre (³/₄ pints) chicken or beef stock
2 tablespoons cooked long-grain rice
1 teaspoon plain flour
2 tablespoons sour cream
4 tablespoons fresh dill
lemon juice to taste
salt and pepper

....

Heat the stock and add the cooked rice. Mix the flour with the sour cream, add a little of the hot soup and return all to the pan. Remove the stalks of the dill and add them – unchopped – to the stock. Leave to simmer for 10 minutes. Chop the rest of the dill and stir in. Add lemon juice to taste. Just before serving, remove the dill stalks, season and reheat without bringing back to the boil.

Sorrel Soup
Zupa Szczawiowa

There are many different versions of sorrel soup. This recipe, from Lithuania, differs from other, more common, sorrel soups in that it contains small chunks of sausage. I grow sorrel in my garden and so have a ready supply most of the year. If you have the space it is an easy and worthwhile vegetable to grow because it is not frequently found in the shops, unless they are specialist greengrocers. Spinach with the addition of lemon juice can be substituted for sorrel in this recipe.

Serves 6

··

> 1.5 litres (2¹/₂ pints) beef stock
> small quantity of vegetables, e.g. carrots, leeks and
>   onions, peeled and diced
> 5-6 dried mushrooms, washed, soaked and diced
> 400 g (14 oz) smoked sausage
> 400 g (14 oz) fresh sorrel
> 300 ml (¹/₂ pint) single cream
> salt and pepper
> 1 tablespoon lemon juice (optional)
> 3-4 egg yolks (optional)

··

Heat the beef stock and add the vegetables and mushrooms. Chop the sausage into small chunks and mix into the stock. Chop the sorrel finely and stir in. Leave to cook gently for 30 minutes. Add the cream, season and stir in the lemon juice if required. Serve at once. If you would prefer a thicker soup, whisk the cream with 3-4 egg yolks and pour in just before serving without bringing back to the boil.

CRAYFISH SOUP
Zupa Rakowa

This is a recipe from Maria Disslowa's *Continental European Cooking* which has many excellent Polish dishes in it. This is one of the most elegant Polish soups – a rich and tasty crayfish consommé garnished with shell 'boats' of crayfish meat, rice, dill and egg.

Serves 8

8 live freshwater crayfish
2.25 litres (4 pints) vegetable stock
25 g (1 oz) parsley, chopped
1 tablespoon dill, chopped
pinch salt
pinch caraway seeds
50 g (2 oz) butter
300 ml (1/2 pint) double cream
1 level tablespoon flour

For stuffing the shells:
50 g (2 oz) rice
40 g (1 1/2 oz) butter
meat from the crayfish
1 egg, separated
1 teaspoon dill, finely chopped

In cool running water, wash the live crayfish. As the shells are going to be used, clean all parts thoroughly until the water runs clear. In a large saucepan bring the stock to the boil and add a pinch each of the parsley and dill, salt and caraway seeds. Plunge the crayfish head-first into the stock and boil for 10 minutes. Remove, retaining the stock, break the claws and tails and take out the meat. Remove the legs and pick the meat from the back shells, leaving the shells whole for stuffing. Take the intestines off the back of the tails and place the tails in a tureen. Keep the remaining meat (from claws and backs) for stuffing. Pound the tail and claw shells in a mortar and fry them in hot butter until all the moisture has evaporated and the shells turn deep red-brown. Add some of the stock in which the crayfish have been cooked, boil for a few minutes and strain into a saucepan. Repeat the process several times, using fresh stock every time, until all the fat is drawn out of the crushed shells and incorporated into the stock.

To stuff the shells, boil the rice with the butter in 300 ml (¹/₂ pint) water until it is thick and soft. Finely chop the crayfish meat from the claws and backs, and mix with the egg yolk, rice and dill. Beat the egg white until stiff, mix into the meat mixture and fill the shells with it.

Bring the stock to the boil, add the stuffed shells and cook for 10 minutes. Lift the shells out and set aside. Blend the cream with the flour and stir into the stock to thicken it. Add the remaining chopped parsley and dill. Pour the soup into a tureen, return the stuffed shells to the soup, and serve at once.

Lithuanian Cold Beetroot Soup
Chłodnik

Different households vary in their preparation of this soup. Crayfish flesh may be added, or strips of roasted veal; and other additions might be roasted roebuck or a big boiled fish, and even florets of cauliflower and asparagus tips. As with the Hunter's Stew on page 165, almost anything can be used. This version is simple and inexpensive, and offers pleasing contrasts in both colour and texture, with crunchy radishes and cucumbers amid the smooth folds of yoghurt, and bright green flecks of dill or chives standing out against the delicate pink background. This is a wholesome and healthy soup, and one of the nicest possible summer tastes.

Serves 4

300 ml (¹/₂ pint) beet juice (the juice from bottled
  pickled beetroot can be used)
300 ml (¹/₂ pint) sour cream
450 ml (³/₄ pint) natural yoghurt
1 cucumber, peeled and diced
2 tablespoons fresh dill, chopped
a little finely grated raw beetroot – just to add colour
2 tablespoons fresh chives, chopped
4 medium-sized radishes, thinly sliced
1 hard-boiled egg

Combine all the ingredients except the egg, and chill in the refrigerator for at least 4 hours before serving, to let the flavours mingle. Just before serving, quarter or slice the hard-boiled egg and arrange it in the soup plates, pour the soup over and serve.

CHILLED WILD STRAWBERRY SOUP
Zimna Zupa Poziomkowa

As in many other Eastern European countries, fruit soups are often served during the summer. Blackcurrants, cherries, plums, strawberries and raspberries all make delicate and aromatic soups and their lightness is well suited to a warm day. Wild strawberries are particularly delicious for soup as they contain just the right amount of tartness needed to prevent the soup becoming sickly. Ordinary strawberries can be used, but lemon juice must also be added to achieve the correct flavour.

Serves 4

> **500 g (1 lb 2 oz) wild strawberries**
> **150 ml (¼ pint) milk**
> **300 ml (½ pint) sour cream sugar to taste**

Wash the fruit, drain and press through a sieve. Stir in the milk and sour cream. Add sugar to taste and chill before serving. This can also be made with raspberries.

COLD CHERRY SOUP
Zimna Zupa Czereśniowa

This is a typical Eastern European fruit soup with a rich body of red wine flavoured with cherries and then delicately dusted with cinnamon. For a less heady alternative, use 750 ml (1¼ pints) of thin sour cream instead of red wine.

Serves 6

> **2.25 litres (4 pints) cherries**
> **pinch cinnamon**
> **2-3 cloves, crushed**
> **300 g (10½ oz) sugar**
> **300 ml (½ pint) red wine**
> **450 ml (¾ pint) water, boiled and cooled**

Crush the cherries, with their stones, add the cinnamon and cloves and leave for several hours in an earthenware vessel, the glaze of which will not react to the acidity of the fruit. Strain through a sieve to remove the stones, then stir in the sugar and wine and dilute with the boiled and cooled water.

GARNISHES FOR SOUPS

CHOUX-PASTE PEAS
Groszek Ptysiowy

This is a good garnish to serve with any thin vegetable or fruit soup.

Serves 4

25 g (1 oz) butter
4¹/₂ tablespoons water
3 level tablespoons flour
1 egg

Melt the butter, add the water and bring to the boil. Stir in the flour over a very low heat until the mixture holds together. Set aside to cool. Mix in the egg until it is thoroughly incorporated, and leave to stand for one hour in a cool place. It should be a little like putty. Break off small pieces of the dough and make pea-size balls. Dust them with flour and place on a lightly greased baking tray. Bake in the oven at 260C/400F/Gas 6 until golden in colour and well risen – approximately 10 minutes. Float some on the top of each bowl of soup.

FRENCH NOODLES
Francuskie Kluski

These noodles are generally served with clear meat stocks such as the juices from Pot Roast Beef (see page 66).

Serves 4

50 g (2 oz) butter
1 egg, separated
100 g (3¹/₂ oz) plain flour
pinch salt

Cream the butter. Whisk the egg yolk and mix into the butter. Beat the egg white until very stiff. Stir the flour into the butter mixture, fold in the egg white and salt, adding more flour if the mixture is not thick enough; the texture must be very firm.

Opposite: Beetroot Soup (*Barszcz*)

Bring the soup to the boil, take teaspoons of the above mixture and drop them into the soup. Run the spoon under cold water from time to time to prevent the dough from sticking. Boil the soup for five minutes and serve.

Egg Drops
Lane Ciasto

This is often served with a good meat stock.

Serves 4

2 eggs
2 generous tablespoons flour

Beat the eggs, slowly adding flour until you have a smooth thickish batter of pouring consistency. Heat the clear soup to boiling point and pour a little of this mixture from quite a height into the soup. It should immediately form ribbon 'noodles'. If the batter dissolves instead of becoming noodles, add a little more flour. Continue with the remaining mixture. Boil the soup for 2-3 minutes, or until the noodles have risen to the surface, and serve.

Opposite: Lenten Herrings (*Postne Śledzie*)

SMALL SUET DUMPLINGS
Pulpety Na Łoju

A traditional accompaniment to tripe, these dumplings can also be served with soup.

Serves 4-6

175 g (6 oz) suet
2 eggs
150 g (5 oz) dried breadcrumbs
50 g (2 oz) plain flour
1 teaspoon salt
$^1/_2$ teaspoon freshly ground pepper
1 teaspoon parsley

Thoroughly mix all the ingredients, kneading by hand to form a smooth dough. Pull off pieces and form plum-sized dumplings. Bring a large pan of salted water to the boil and test one of the dumplings by dropping it into the water and simmering for 7-8 minutes. If it holds together, remove from the water and spoon in the remaining dumplings to cook. If it crumbles, knead the mixture for a further 5 minutes and then try again.

Remove the cooked dumplings carefully with a slotted spoon and serve immediately.

HORS D'OEUVRES

In Poland there are two types of hors d'oeuvre, *kanapki* (canapés), which are tiny open sandwiches similar to those found in the Scandinavian smorgasbord, and the more substantial *zakąski* (starters), which are more like what we think of as hors d'oeuvres. At a meal in a restaurant, one will be offered *zakąski,* which include little dumplings, stuffed eggs, a cold chicken or fish dish in aspic, pancakes or bliny, pâté, and probably several versions of pickled herring. These will be followed by a main course of game or fish or other meats. At a private house, however, one might well be served *kanapki,* accompanied by vodka, before a meal. These are small squares of dark or light rye bread on which lie a variety of spreads, such as herring, or hard-boiled eggs chopped finely and mixed with mustard and gherkins, or tiny pickled mushrooms. There are no standard formats for these snacks and they will simply reflect what is available in the shops and what is affordable. Caviar, for example, is easy to buy in the free markets but beyond the purchasing power of most people, although for those with hard currency it is about a quarter of the price one would pay for it in Britain. Among the following recipes there are also two – Little Fingers (*paluszki*) and Cheese Pastries (*paluszki serowe*) – which conform far more to what the British expect to accompany drinks.

Hors d'oeuvres have two differing roles in Polish cuisine: they may be either a supplement to a meal or a meal in themselves. Very often the dishes that grace the evening table will be the classic *zakąski*, and may include herrings in sour cream, a plate of smoked sausage, and probably the very mild soft white Polish cheese which is sprinkled with salt and eaten on rye bread. Hot dishes might be fried or boiled dumplings, stuffed pancakes or little sauerkraut pastries. The meal would then finish with a sweet cake and coffee.

HERRING WITH APPLES
Śledzie z Jabłkami i Chrzanem

There is no lack of herring in Poland, as it is fished in large quantities in the Baltic Sea to the north of the country. There are many different herring dishes, and although they can of course be eaten fresh, the most favoured way of preparing them is to fillet them and marinate them in vinegar, normally with onions. In this form they are then mixed with sour cream or horseradish, garnished with anchovies, eggs, tomatoes or even apples as in this recipe.

Serves 2

> 6 salted herring fillets
> 400 g (14 oz) apples (sweet red ones are most suitable)
> 1¹/₂ teaspoons horseradish cream
> pinch of sugar
> 2 tomatoes, sliced

Rinse the herrings and reserve. Peel and grate the apples coarsely. Add the horseradish cream and sugar and mix well. Put a layer of the apples on a salad dish, roll the herrings into bundles and place on top of the apples. Place a slice of tomato between each herring, and serve.

HERRING SPREAD
Pasta Śledziowa

Serves 4

> 2 fresh herrings, filleted
> 50 g (2 oz) butter to each 25 g (1 oz) of fish

Pound the raw fish to a smooth paste with a pestle and mortar. Gradually incorporate the butter, which should be well softened. Force the mixture through a sieve, spoon into ramekins and chill until needed.
This should be served with rye bread.

HERRING WITH SOUR CREAM
Śledzie w Śmietanie

Herring is a traditional Polish hors d'oeuvre, and is served in various ways. It is normally accompanied by small glasses of ice-cold vodka, which are drunk in one gulp, and which perfectly suit the saltiness of the herring.

Serves 4

> **12 salted herring fillets**
> **100 g (3¹/₂ oz) onion**
> **4 hard-boiled eggs**
> **250 ml (scant ¹/₂ pint) sour cream**

Rinse the herrings and set aside. Peel the onion and cut into rings. Divide the onion rings between four plates. Halve the eggs and place face downwards on the onions. Coil the herrings up tightly and place on either side of and between the eggs – three to a plate. Stir the sour cream thoroughly, spoon over the herrings, and chill.

COLD STUFFED EGGS
Nadziewane Jajka

Serves 6

> **6 eggs, hard-boiled**
> **salt and pepper**
> **1 level teaspoon French mustard**

Peel the hard-boiled eggs and cut them in half. Remove the yolks and mash them until fluffy with the mustard. Season to taste. Replace in the hollows of the whites and serve.

Hot Stuffed Eggs
Faszerowane Jajka

Serves 6

> 6 eggs, hard-boiled
> 1 tablespoon minced parsley
> 1 tablespoon chives, or the green tops of spring onions,
>   chopped finely
> 2 tablespoons single cream
> salt and pepper
> 25-50 g (1-2 oz) dried white breadcrumbs

Cut the eggs lengthways with a very sharp knife, taking care not to break the shells. Scoop out the eggs and mix with the parsley, chives and cream. Season well. Push the mixture back into the shells and sprinkle a thick layer of breadcrumbs on top, Grill, or fry upside down.

Little Fingers
Paluszki

This makes a delicious accompaniment to drinks, and are best served straight from the oven.

Serves 4

> 125 g (4¹/₂ oz) butter
> 125 g (4¹/₂ oz) cooked potato, mashed
> 125 g (4¹/₂ oz) flour
> 1 egg, beaten
> salt
> 1 tablespoon caraway seeds

Preheat the oven to 240C/475F/Gas 9. Combine the butter, potato and flour to make a dough, turn on to a well-floured board and knead. Refrigerate for 15 minutes, then roll out very thinly. Cut into narrow strips. Place on a well-greased baking tray and brush with beaten egg. Sprinkle with salt and caraway seeds. Bake for approximately 10 minutes, until golden.

HARE PÂTÉ
Pasztet z Zalqca

As game is abundant in Poland, pâtés such as this one are often made. A bread roll is used here since this is the normal form of soft white bread available in Poland.

Serves 6

Hind and fore-quarters of a hare
2 carrots
2 onions, peeled
1 bunch parsley
1 handful dried mushrroms, washed and soaked
1-2 bay leaves
$1/2$ teaspoon ground allspice
$1/4$ teaspoon grated nutmeg
salt and black pepper
50 g (2 oz) lard
250 g (9 oz) liver, from the hare, supplemented
    with calves' or pigs' liver
4 eggs, beaten
1 white bread roll
salt and pepper
$1/4$ teaspoon grated nutmeg
$1/4$ teaspoon ground ginger
lard for greasing
300 g ($10^1/2$ oz) pork back fat, sliced

Preheat the oven to 200C/400F/Gas 6. Put the meat into a large pan with the carrots and onions, left whole, parsley, mushrooms and seasonings. Add water to cover and simmer for 40 minutes. Remove the meat and lard it with a larding needle. Return to the pan and simmer for a further 30 minutes, until tender. Strain the stock, discarding the vegetables. Bone the meat and return to the stock. Leave to cool.

Slice the liver and cook in a little water for 5 minutes. Add the liver and the eggs to the stock and meat, and blend well. Soak the bread roll in water for 10 minutes, squeeze out and add to the pâté. Blend again, and season with salt, pepper, nutmeg and ginger. Grease the bottom of a terrine dish with lard, and line with the slices of pork back fat. Pour the pâté mixture into the dish; it should be three-quarters full.

Fill a roasting dish with boiling water, stand the terrine dish in it so that the water comes three-quarters of the way up the sides. Bake, covered, until cooked – approximately $2^1/2$ hours.

Chicken in Aspic
Kura w Galarecie

Serves 6

....

1 kg (2¹/₄ lb) whole chicken or chicken joints
2 onions, peeled
2 carrots, scraped and sliced
1 parsnip, scraped and sliced
4-5 peppercorns
4-5 allspice berries
2 hard-boiled eggs, sliced
300 g (10¹/₂ oz) petits pois, cooked
3 x 11 g (0.4 oz) sachets of gelatine
juice of 1 lemon

....

Put the chicken into a large pan together with the whole onions, carrots, parsnip and seasonings. Cover with cold water, bring to the boil and simmer until the chicken is done – approximately 2 hours for a whole bird, 15-20 minutes for joints. Remove the chicken and retain the stock. When cool, joint the chicken if necessary and chop the meat finely. Take a large rectangular dish and in it lay the slices of hard-boiled egg and sprinkle over the *petits pois*. Remove the vegetables from the stock and lay half on top of the *petits pois*. Spread the chopped chicken over the vegetables, and cover with the remaining vegetables.

Dissolve the gelatine in hot stock, mix in the lemon juice and pour over the chicken. Put in the refrigerator and chill for at least 3 hours until set. Just before serving, run a hot knife around the edges of the dish and turn upside down onto a serving dish.

CHEESE PASTRIES
Paluszki Serowe

Like the 'little fingers' above, these are good to have with drinks.

Serves 4

50 g (2 oz) flour
50 g (2 oz) butter, cut into pieces
50 g (2 oz) Parmesan cheese, grated
pinch paprika
pinch salt
water to mix
1 egg, beaten

Preheat the oven to 200C/400F/Gas 6. Put flour, butter, cheese, paprika and salt into a bowl and rub in the butter; add a little water if necessary to make a firm, smooth dough. Leave for an hour. Roll out thinly, cut into fancy shapes and glaze with the beaten egg. Bake for 10 minutes. Serve warm.

ASPARAGUS À LA POLONAISE
Szparagi po Polsku

The asparagus grown in Poland is the green variety, as in England.

Serves 4

1 kg (2¹/₄ lb) fresh asparagus
2 teaspoons salt
1 teaspoon sugar
50 g (2 oz) butter
25 g (1 oz) dried white breadcrumbs

Scrape the stems of the asparagus and trim the woody base of each. Wash well and tie into bundles with similar-sized stalks together. Bring a large pan of water to the boil, season it with sugar and salt, and add the asparagus. Cook, depending on the thickness of the stems, until tender. (Pierce the base of the stalks with a knife to see if they are done.) Drain, separate and place on a suitable dish.

Brown the butter over a medium heat without letting it burn, stir in the breadcrumbs and pour over the asparagus. Serve at once.

Asparagus Pudding
Budyń ze Szparagów

This is a deliciously tasty soufflé.

Serves 4

....

250 g (9 oz) fresh asparagus
pinch salt
pinch sugar
150 ml (¹/₄ pint) milk
40 g (1¹/₂ oz) butter
50 g (2 oz) flour
3 eggs, separated

For the garnish:
50 g (2 oz) melted butter
2 dessertspoons stale white breadcrumbs

....

Rinse the asparagus, scrape and trim and drop into boiling water, seasoned with salt and sugar. When cooked, drain and cut the tender part of the asparagus into chunks 2.5 cm (1 in) long. Discard the woody stems.

In a pan bring the milk and butter to the boil, pour in the flour and mix very quickly to achieve a smooth sauce. Cook over a gentle heat until the mixture holds together and leaves the sides of the pan clean. Pour into a large bowl and beat in the egg yolks one by one. Mix for 10 minutes. Whisk the egg whites until very stiff and fold into the dough.

Stir in the asparagus, and pour the mixture into a suitable greased dish with a cover. Stand the dish in a large tin or container of simmering water and cook over a medium heat for 45 minutes, allowing the water to simmer gently.

Test to see if the pudding is cooked by inserting a knife into the middle; if it comes away moist, leave to cook until the knife comes away clean. Remove from the dish and cut into slices. Pour over the melted butter mixed with breadcrumbs, and serve.

PANCAKES WITH MEAT
Paszteciki

These pancakes are also excellent with a filling of liver, mushrooms and onion, and can be served with a tomato or mushroom sauce or as an accompaniment to soup.

For the pancakes:
150 g (5 oz) plain flour
1 egg
1 egg yolk
1 tablespoon melted butter
salt and pepper
300 ml (1/2 pint) milk
oil for frying

For the filling:
2 large onions, peeled
50 g (2 oz) butter
450 g (1 lb) pork, beef or chicken, cooked and minced
salt and pepper
1 egg, beaten

For the coating:
1 egg
25-50 g (1-2 oz) dried breadcrumbs
butter for frying

To make the pancakes, sift the flour into the bowl, add the egg, egg yolk, butter, seasonings and half the milk. Whisk until smooth. Add the remaining milk, whisk again and set aside for 1 hour. Heat a heavy frying pan with just enough oil to cover the bottom. When it is hot, pour off the oil into a heatproof container, and pour in sufficient batter to cover the base of the pan very thinly. When the batter has set and is browned underneath, toss and cook on the other side. Continue until all the batter has been used.

To make the filling, dice the onions and fry in the butter until golden. Add the minced meat, stir well and season. Remove from the heat and stir in the beaten egg to bind.

Lay the pancakes out on a board, slightly overlapping each other, and spoon the filling horizontally down the centre of the pancakes. Roll the pancakes up lengthways to make one long roll. Cut 5 cm (2 in) slices off this at an angle.

For the coating, beat the egg in a shallow bowl, and sprinkle the breadcrumbs on a flat plate. Dip the pancake pieces into the egg and then coat well with breadcrumbs, shaking off the excess. Melt the butter in a frying pan and fry the pancakes on both sides until golden. Serve at once.

BLINIS

These Russian yeast pancakes are now internationally known. Most often served with a layer of sour cream topped with caviar, they can be eaten with any savoury filling and sprinkled with hard-boiled egg. They can also be eaten as a dessert, with jam or lemon juice accompanied by sugar and sour cream.

Makes 4 large blinis

....

120 g (4¼ oz) plain or buckwheat flour
12½ g (½ oz) fresh yeast or 6 g (¼ oz) dried yeast
1 teaspoon sugar
300 ml (½ pint) milk
1 egg, beaten
pinch salt
lard for frying

....

Sift the flour and mix 1 tablespoon of it with the yeast and sugar. Warm the milk to blood heat and stir into the yeast mixture enough to make a smooth liquid batter – it should have the consistency of single cream. Leave to rise in a warm place for 15 minutes.

Add the remaining milk to the rest of the flour and mix well. incorporate the egg and salt. When the yeast mixture is risen and frothy, whisk it into the rest and leave to rise again in a warm place for 40 minutes.

Heat a heavy iron frying pan smeared with a little fat, and when very hot pour in enough batter just to cover the bottom of the pan. Cook quickly on both sides. Put the cooked blinis in a warm oven while the others are being cooked.

Serve with sour cream and caviar.

WHITE CHEESE PATTIES
Mądrzyki

I found this delicious recipe in Mrs Cielecka's own recipe book, which was started before the Second World War and contains some wonderful dishes. It is like a calendar of events, as one reads items varying from exquisite recipes to ideas on coping with rationing or common illnesses associated with lack of proper nourishment. This piece of culinary history has already been 'bagged' by her youngest granddaughter, much to Mrs Cielecka's amusement.

Serves 4

250 g (9 oz) soft white cheese (curd cheese is suitable)
2 eggs
pinch salt
50 g (2 oz) butter
100 g (3¹/₂ oz) flour
flour for dusting
butter for frying
butter, melted
sour cream

Mash the cheese and mix with the eggs, salt and butter. Stir in the flour to make a stiff mixture. With wet hands, form small patties about 6 cm (2¹/₂ in) round. Dust lightly in flour and fry in butter until golden on both sides. Serve with melted butter and sour cream.

DUMPLINGS STUFFED WITH MEAT
Kopytka Nadziewane Mięsem

Serves 4

50 g (2 oz) onion, peeled
25 g (1 oz) butter
250 g (9 oz) minced meat, cooked
salt and pepper
500 g (1 lb 2 oz) potatoes, cooked and mashed
1 egg, beaten

100 g (3¹/₂ oz) flour
sour cream

Dice the onion and fry in the butter until golden. Add the meat to the onion and season, mixing well. Remove from the heat and reserve.

To make the dumplings, put the potatoes in a large bowl, add the egg and flour and mix to form a dough, adding more flour if it is too sticky. Make the dough into a roll and cut into thin slices. Fill each piece with the meat mixture, fold the edges and roll in your hands to make a ball. Boil in salted water for about 5 minutes. Drain and serve with sour cream.

LAZY DUMPLINGS
Leniwe Pierogi

The name for these dumplings relates to their being unfilled, unlike the other varieties of Polish dumplings containing mushroom, cabbage or meat. The flavouring – of cheese – is incorporated in the dough, thereby reducing the work!

Serves 4

---

225 g (8 oz) curd cheese
1-2 tablespoons milk
¹/₂ teaspoon sugar
¹/₂ teaspoon salt
1 egg, separated
175 g (6 oz) plain flour
2 tablespoons breadcrumbs made from stale
**   white or brown bread**
25 g (1 oz) butter

Soften the cheese with the milk in a bowl. Sprinkle on the sugar and salt, and mix in the egg yolk until well absorbed. Beat the egg white until just stiff and fold into the mixture. Fold in half the flour. Spread a thick layer of flour on a marble board and turn the mixture on to this, working more flour into it and kneading well until the dough does not stick to your fingers. Make into a long roll, approximately 2.5 cm (1 in) wide, and flatten slightly with a knife. Cut diagonally into 3-5 cm (1¹/₂-2 in) pieces and cook in plenty of boiling salted water. When they rise to the surface, let them boil for a further 2-3 minutes and then drain.

Melt the butter, fry the breadcrumbs and pour over the dumplings.

SAUERKRAUT PASTIES
Kapuśniaczki

Serves 4

50 g (2 oz) butter
1 onion, peeled
450 g (1 lb) sauerkraut
1 handful dried mushrooms, washed and soaked
4 medium-sized flat mushrooms
400 g (14 oz) rich yeast pastry (see page 154)
1 egg, beaten

Preheat the oven to 200C/400F/Gas 6. Melt the butter in a pan, chop the onion and fry until golden. Rinse the sauerkraut and add to the pan, dice all the mushrooms and mix in, together with a drop of water.

Roll the pastry out fairly thinly, into a large rectangle. Cut into squares 10 cm x 10 cm (4 in x 4 in) and fill each with a spoonful of sauerkraut. Fold the corners in and seal with beaten egg to form little parcels. Brush with beaten egg and bake in the preheated oven for 45 minutes until golden-brown.

STUFFED KOHLRABI
Kalarepa Nadziewana

Kohlrabi are normally eaten stuffed in Poland, either with meat as below or with crayfish and green dill.

Serves 4

4 young kohlrabi
450 g (1 lb) minced, cooked lamb, pork or veal
2 tablespoons dried white breadcrumbs
2 eggs
2 tablespoons chopped parsley
salt and pepper
600-1200 ml (1-2 pints) meat stock
50 g (2 oz) butter
2 tablespoons flour

Cut off the tops of the kohlrabi to make little caps. Peel and hollow out the bases, discarding the flesh. Combine the meat with the breadcrumbs, eggs, parsley, salt and pepper. Mix well and fill the kohlrabi. Replace the caps firmly, tying with cotton to secure them. Put into a large fireproof casserole dish and pour in the stock; it should come to just beneath the openings on the kohlrabi. Cover the dish and braise on a medium heat for 30 minutes.

When the kohlrabi are soft, melt the butter in a separate pan, add the flour and allow to brown a little. Incorporate some of the stock from the kohlrabi, to make a sauce with the consistency of double cream.

To serve, arrange the kohlrabi on a suitable plate and pour the thickened stock over.

Pierogi with Meat in Rich Yeast Pastry
Pierogi z Mięsem z Ciasta Drożdżowego

Serves 4

50 g (2 oz) butter
6 button mushrooms, sliced
1 tablespoon chopped onion
1 tablespoon flour
300 ml (¹/₂ pint) chicken stock
50 g (2 oz) veal, minced
2 chicken livers, finely chopped
1 hard-boiled egg, finely chopped
salt and pepper
400 g (14 oz) rich yeast pastry (see page 154)
a little milk to glaze

Preheat the oven to 190C/375F/Gas 5. Melt the butter in a pan, add the mushrooms and onion, and just before they begin to brown add the flour. Add the stock and veal, the chicken livers, the hard-boiled egg, salt and pepper. Cook over a low heat until the stock has been reduced and the mixture has barely any liquid left.

Roll out the pastry dough thinly and cut it into circles the diameter of a small saucer. On each circle put a spoonful of meat. Fold the dough over to form crescents and pinch the open edges with the back of a fork. Brush the tops with milk and bake for 40 minutes until golden-brown and well risen.

FISH AND SHELLFISH

Of the types of fish available in Poland, freshwater fish predominate. Crayfish, eel, perch, salmon, sturgeon, tench and trout can all be found, but the favourites are carp and pike, and it is these two that are served on special occasions and traditionally make an appearance on the table at dinner on Christmas Eve.

The Baltic provides the country with cod, herring and plaice. Herring is the most useful of fish, being so well suited to pickling. Marinated and preserved in vinegar, with onions, peppercorns and bay leaves, it can be eaten all year round and, as in Russia and Scandinavia, is a popular hors d'oeuvre (see pages 28-29). Neither cod nor plaice are eaten much, the various river fish being found preferable.

Although Poles have an unhealthy liking for meat, fish has played an essential part in the Polish diet since the tenth century when Catholicism was accepted in Poland, and the Catholic tradition of not eating meat on fast days has been followed ever since. Fish is substituted for meat on Fridays, fast days throughout the calendar and at special feasts such as dinner on Christmas Eve. Without a doubt, compared with meat, fish is considered second best, but due culinary attention has been paid to it, and there are some wonderful Polish fish dishes. Whereas during Lent and on other fast days, herring would normally be served, accompanied by baked potatoes, without their skins and without any butter, on meatless feast days a more exotic preparation was allowed. Carp and pike, two of the ugliest fish, make quite sensational dishes as, for example, Stuffed Carp with a Mushroom Sauce (see page 44), or Pike in Polish Sauce (see page 42), where the sweetness of the fish is married brilliantly with a wine vinegar and raisin sauce.

With the advent of big supermarkets and their fresh fish counters, buying fish today is a far more pleasant experience than when I first came to live in Poland in 1991. I remember standing in a queue and watching the woman in front of me having the fish of her choice being netted in the tank. It was then wrapped up in brown paper and handed to her with its head still thrashing from side to side.

PIKE

In the first printed edition of the recipes of Paweł Tremo, chef to King Stanisław August Poniatowski (Cracow, 1839), there are some exquisite dishes. Sadly, these recipes are no longer in print, but they have been kept for posterity in the library of the Jagiellonian University in Cracow. Looking down the list of contents would keep many a gourmand happy, and amused by such dishes as *Pike with anchovy sauce, when the fish is not too fresh*. Below are two recipes for cooking *fresh* pike, from this collection.

GRILLED PIKE
Szczupak z Rożna

Trim and dress the pike, then sprinkle it with salt and leave it for about one hour. Afterwards rub off the salt and pat the pike dry. Clarify some butter and spread it over the pike, placing it under a low grill. Grill the pike, repeatedly turning it over and covering with butter.

PIKE WITH NATURAL SAUCE
Szczupak w Sosie Naturalnym

'Shave' the pike, trim it and sprinkle with salt, leaving for some time. The fresher the fish, the less time it needs to lie in the salt. Take some parsnips, some onions and chop them, placing them in a saucepan covered with water. When the vegetables are half cooked, rinse the pike and place it with the vegetables. When the fish is half cooked, take some butter and one tablespoon of flour and mix it well, adding some water. Cook it, mixing all the time until the taste of flour disappears. Add some chopped parsley and some pepper to the sauce and bring it to the boil. Pour the sauce over the hot pike just before serving. You can also serve this sauce with sea bass, carp, tench, bream or small fish.

PIKE IN POLISH SAUCE
Szczupak w Szarym Sosie

Serves 4

900 g (2 lb) pike steak, cleaned
1/2 bottle dry white wine
125 ml (scant 1/4 pint) white wine vinegar
2 tablespoons seedless raisins
25 g (1 oz) butter
1 tablespoon flour
1 teaspoon sugar

Wash and dry the pike and put into a fish kettle or saucepan with the wine, vinegar and raisins. Poach gently for 30 minutes, remove the fish and keep warm.

Melt the butter in a saucepan and stir in the flour. Gradually add the liquid in which the fish was cooked and stir in the sugar at the end. Bring to the boil and stir continuously until the sauce is smooth and thoroughly blended. Skin the pike, remove the bone if you like, and arrange on plates. Pour over the sauce and serve at once.

CARP

Carp is considered a noble fish in poland, where it has been bred for eating since the thirteenth century. It is probably the most popular fish in Polish cooking (with pike not far behind). Although available all year round, it is actually at its best in winter, and is traditionally eaten – in one form or another – on Christmas Eve.

If you have the good fortune to have fresh, live carp, you will need to clear the muddy taste that is common to carp; to do this, put the live fish in a bucket or basin of water and change the water 3 or 4 times over the course of 24 hours. Alexandre Durnas suggested an alternative way:

> Make the fish which has just been taken from the water, drink a glass of strong vinegar and at the very instant you will see a sort of thick perspiration spread itself over its whole body, which you will remove by scaling it. When it is dead, its flesh will become firm and have as good a taste as if it had been caught in running water.

It is more common nowadays, however, to buy carp from the fishmonger, in which case they should be scaled, cleaned and left to soak for 3-4 hours in slightly salted water.

KING'S CARP
Karp po Królewsku

This recipe is taken from a cookbook by Wojciech Wieladko, which was published in Warsaw in 1800:

> Bone the fish and chop the meat finely. Add to it herbs, słonina [pork fat], mushrooms, parsley and onions and fry it together. Combine with a few hard-boiled egg yolks, salt, pepper, mushrooms and milk.
>
> When it cools down, form the mixture into a fish shape, then coat with beaten egg yolks and sprinkle breadcrumbs on top. Bake in the oven and serve hot.

STUFFED CARP WITH A MUSHROOM SAUCE
Karp Nadziewany w Sosie Grzybowym

This is a wonderfully delicate dish, full of flavour and beautifully light. A variation on the theme without the use of animal fats could probably be seen on the Christmas dinner table. Since in Poland the softest white bread is to be found in rolls, the inside of a roll is used in the recipe for the stuffing.

Serves 6

....

1 carp, weighing approx. 1 kg 350 g (3 lb),
    cleaned and scaled
salt and pepper
2 carrots, thinly sliced
2 sticks celery, thinly sliced
knob of butter for cooking

For the stuffing:
50 g (2 oz) butter
100 g (¹/₂ oz) button mushrooms
2 eggs, separated
1 small white bread roll
150 ml (¹/₄ pint) milk
1 tablespoon chopped parsley
salt and pepper

For the mushroom sauce:
25 g (1 oz) butter
1 onion, peeled and diced
100 g (3¹/₂ oz) flat mushrooms
salt and pepper
25 g (1 oz) plain flour
scant 75 ml (3 fl oz) fish or vegetable stock
scant 75 ml (3 fl oz) dry white wine
scant 75 ml (3 fl oz) single cream
juice of ¹/₂ lemon
2 egg yolks

....

Rinse the carp, season well and leave for 30 minutes for the seasoning to flavour the flesh. Grease an ovenproof dish and lay the slices of carrot and celery on the bottom.

Preheat the oven to 180C/350F/Gas 4. To prepare the stuffing, melt half the butter in a pan, chop the mushrooms into small slices and stew. Leave to cool. Cream the rest of the butter in a bowl, adding the two egg yolks one after the other. Remove the crust of the roll and soak the inside in milk until soft. Squeeze out the bread, discarding the milk, and mix with the butter and yolks. Stir in the cold mushrooms, the parsley, and seasoning to taste. Beat the egg whites until very stiff and fold in. Spoon the stuffing into the fish and sew up or secure with a toothpick.

Place the fish on top of the vegetables in the ovenproof dish. Put a piece of butter on top and bake for 30 minutes, basting the fish with its juices several times.

Meanwhile, make the sauce. Melt the butter and fry the onion until golden. Cut the mushrooms into thick slices, mix with the onion, season and stew until soft. Sprinkle the mushroom mixture with flour, add the stock, wine and cream and allow to boil for a few minutes. Stir in the lemon juice, take the sauce off the heat and mix in the egg yolks. Arrange the carp on a serving dish, pour the sauce over, and serve immediately.

POACHED CARP WITH ROE SAUCE
Karp w Sosie Ikrouym

Serves 8

For the stock:
2 carrots
1 onion
1 leek
1 bunch parsley
salt and pepper
1 litre (1³/₄ pints) water

1.8 kg (4 lb) carp, cleaned and scaled, with roe
salt
25 g (1 oz) butter
1 bay leaf
5 black peppercorns
4 juniper berries
500 ml (scant 1 pint) dry white wine
1 tablespoon white wine vinegar
handful dried mushrooms, washed and soaked,
**   or 200 g (7 oz) fresh flat mushrooms**
50 g (2 oz) butter
1 tablespoon flour
2 tablespoons sour cream

1 egg yolk
pinch paprika or 1 teaspoon soy sauce

....

Combine the ingredients for the stock, bring to the boil and simmer for 30 minutes. Rinse the carp, remove and reserve the roe, and sprinkle the fish with salt. Leave for 30 minutes. Rinse well and put in a fish kettle or saucepan. Add the butter and pour on the vegetable stock. Add the bay leaf, peppercorns, juniper berries and white wine. Cover the pan and leave to cook on a low heat for 20-25 minutes, basting frequently. Retain the stock and keep the fish warm.

Pour 125 ml (¼ pint) boiling water, mixed with 1 tablespoon of vinegar, on to the roe. Bring to the boil and cook for a few minutes. Cut the mushrooms into thin strips. Cube the cooked roe and braise with the mushrooms in half the butter.

In another saucepan, melt the rest of the butter, stir in the flour and cook gently for a minute or two. Gradually add enough stock from the fish to make a smooth sauce with the consistency of single cream. Whisk in the sour cream, egg yolk, paprika or soy sauce. Stir in the roe and mushrooms.

Put the carp on a serving plate, pour a little of the sauce over it, and pass the rest round separately in a sauceboat.

SALMON À LA POLONAISE
Łosoś po Polsku

Serves 6

....

1 kg (2¼ lb) salmon in one piece, skin removed
100 g (3½ oz) bacon slices
1 teaspoon salt
juice of 1 lemon
150 ml (¼ pint) dry white wine
50 g (2 oz) butter
1 tablespoon flour

....

Preheat the oven to 220C/425F/Gas 7. Cut one slice of bacon into narrow strips and, using a larding needle, thread the strips through the top of the fish. Rub the fish with salt, wrap the rest of the bacon round it and secure with thread. Bake for 15 minutes. Baste with the lemon juice and wine and return to the oven for a further 10 minutes.

Melt the butter, stir in the flour to make a roux, gradually add the liquid from the roasting tin and bring to the boil. Simmer for 5 minutes.

To serve, remove the thread from the salmon and pour the sauce over the fish.

STURGEON WITH CREAM AND DILL
Jesiotr w Sosie Śmietanowo-koperkowym

This fish, which is best known for giving us caviar, has firm and tasty flesh. Its skin, though, is very hard and must be removed before cooking.

Serves 4

900 g (2 lb) piece of sturgeon, cleaned and skinned
1 onion, peeled
1 carrot
1 parsnip
1 stick celery
salt and pepper
25 g (1 oz) butter
1 tablespoon plain flour
500 ml (scant 1 pint) double cream
3 tablespoons fresh green dill, chopped

Fill a fish kettle with water and add the whole onion, carrot, parsnip, celery and the sturgeon. Season. Poach gently until the fish is soft. Remove the fish, discarding the vegetables but reserving the stock, and keep warm.

Melt the butter in a saucepan and add the flour to make a roux. Gradually mix in a little of the liquid in which the fish was cooked until the sauce has the consistency of single cream. Add the cream and dill, bring to the boil and pour over the sturgeon.

Serve with noodles or buckwheat (see page 89).

ROAST EEL
Węgorz Pieczony

This delicious and underestimated fish, which sounds so much more appealing under its Latin name *Anguilla Anguilla*, is considered a delicacy in Poland. It is eaten either as a starter or as a main course and served in a variety of ways such as smoked, with dill sauce (see page 115), in aspic, marinated, or even soaked in vodka and flambéed. This recipe shows eel at its best: the soft delicate flesh, so at odds with its muscular appearance, is delicious lightly roasted, and well complemented by the mild mustard sauce.

Serves 2

....

> 1 medium eel, skinned and head removed
> salt
> 1 carrot
> 1 parsnip
> 1 onion, peeled
> 1 bunch parsley
> butter
> salt and pepper
> pinch of dill

....

Preheat the oven to 180C/350F/Gas 4. Wash the eel in several changes of water and cut into slices approximately 2.5 cm (1 in) thick. Sprinkle with salt. In a large pan bring some water to the boil and add the eel, the vegetables, left whole, and parsley. Simmer for 20 minutes. Remove the eel from the water, clean off any traces of skin or fat and, if desired, remove the bone. Place the portions of eel on a lightly buttered ovenproof dish, season with salt, pepper and dill, and roast in the oven for 30 minutes.

Serve with mustard sauce (see page 119).

TENCH BRAISED WITH VEGETABLES
Lin Duszony w Jarzynach

This smaller member of the carp family is very difficult to scale. It is therefore best to ask the fishmonger to scale, clean and fillet the fish for you. Otherwise, pouring boiling water on a tench will help to scale it.

Serves 4

900 g (2 lb) tench, cleaned, scaled and filleted
salt and pepper
100 g (3¹/₂ oz) butter
1 onion, peeled
1 stick celery
1 carrot
110 g (4 oz) flat mushrooms

Cut the fish into slices about 2.5 cm (1 in) wide and sprinkle with salt and pepper. Leave for a few hours.

Melt a tablespoon of butter in a flameproof casserole. Pour boiling water over the peeled onion to blanch it, and then slice it, together with the celery and carrot, and add to the casserole. Gently cook the mushrooms in a tablespoon of the butter and add them to the casserole as well. Place the slices of tench in with the vegetables, add the remaining butter and braise on a low heat for 30 minutes. When the fish is soft, serve with the vegetables.

MARZENA'S TROUT
Pstrąg à la Marzena

A friend of mine, Marzena Czubowicz, showed me how to cook this and in fact called it Trout, Warsaw Style, but I always think of it as 'Marzena's Trout'.

Trout in Poland is supposed to be particularly good from the rivers of the Carpathian Mountains in the south of the country.

Serves 6

....

> 6 river trout, skinned and filleted (your fishmonger
>   will do this for you)
> 50 g (2 oz) butter
> 3 medium-sized onions, peeled and diced
> 450 g (1 lb) flat mushrooms
> 2-3 tablespoons plain flour
> juice of 1 lemon
> salt and pepper
> 300 ml (1/2 pint) sour cream

....

Rinse the trout fillets well under cold water and cut into approximately 2.5 cm (1 in) pieces. Melt the butter and fry the diced onions until soft. Chop the mushrooms coarsely and add to the onions. Cook over a medium heat, until the mushrooms have produced some juice.

Toss the fish in the flour and add to the onions and mushrooms, stirring carefully. Add lemon juice and seasoning. When the fish is cooked – this should only take a few minutes – remove the pan from the heat and stir in the sour cream. Serve at once.

FISH IN ASPIC
Ryba Faszerowana

This is often served as an hors d'oeuvre on a special occasion. Rolls are used in the stuffing as they are the normal form of soft white bread available in Poland.

Serves 4 as a main course, 8 as a starter

....

1 large Spanish onion, peeled and chopped
25 g (1 oz) butter
3 white rolls
150 ml (¼ pint) milk
1 kg (2¼ lb) firm white fish fillets, such as sole,
   cod or plaice, skinned and roughly chopped
1 egg yolk
50 ml (2 fl oz) water
pinch each salt, pepper, nutmeg and ginger
handful of vegetables, e.g. 2 carrots, 1 onion,
   1 bunch parsley
1 litre (1¾ pints) water
salt and pepper
1 lemon
1 x 11 g (0.4 oz) sachet of gelatine

You will also need a piece of muslin measuring
   roughly 50 x 50 cm (20 x 20 in)

....

Melt the butter and fry the onion in it until transparent. Take the crust off the rolls and soak the crumb in the milk until soft. Squeeze out the milk and put the bread in a blender with the onion and fish. Mix until very smooth. Remove from the blender and add the egg yolk, water and seasonings. Soak the muslin in cold water and lay it flat. Spread the fish mixture out in two lines (about 25 cm (10 in) long and 7.5 cm (3 in) wide) at each end of the muslin. Roll up the muslin tightly, so the 2 rolls meet in the middle side by side.

Peel and chop the carrots, onion and parsley, and scatter on the bottom of a large flameproof casserole dish. On top of these lay the fish rolls and then pour on 1 litre (1¾ pints) of cold water – it should cover the muslin. Add salt and pepper. Leave to simmer for 1½ hours on top of the stove.

Turn off the heat and leave to cool slightly. Take the fish from the pan, reserving the stock, remove from the muslin and arrange in a fairly deep serving dish. Cut the fish diagonally to produce 4 portions from each line. Slice the lemon and place between each portion of fish. On top of the fish, arrange carrots from the stock, cutting them into pretty shapes. Strain the stock, reheat, and sprinkle the gelatine on to it. Stir until completely dissolved. Pour over the fish and leave for several hours or overnight to set.

POULTRY

Fresh chicken and delicious smoked chicken can be found at butchers, supermarkets and is even sold on street corners by *babys* (literally 'old grandmothers', but a frequently used pejorative word meaning 'old peasant women') in aprons and gaily coloured headscarves.

The chickens sold privately are brought in from the countryside and have a strong, almost gamey flavour, rather similar to the English guinea fowl. This is the authentic chicken so rarely found in England, even among those of the free-range variety.

The favourite Polish way of preparing birds such as chicken, duck and turkey is to stuff them with a liver, bread and onion mixture and then roast them. There are, of course, other methods but none as universally popular as this. Neither goose nor turkey is regarded as an everyday meat and both are only bought for special celebrations such as Christmas and Easter.

THE FIRST SECRET OF THE CHEF

This is a recipe by Stanislaw Czerniecki, a well-known eighteenth century Polish cookery writer, from his book *Compendium Ferculorum* which was published in 1753.

> You need 1 capon which has to be cleaned and trimmed. Skin very carefully, making sure you do not make any holes. If the skin holds tightly to some bones, cut the bones off at that point, so that some of the bones are left with the skin. Put the skin into a big bottle with a neck three fingers wide and hold the skin at the neck. Mix 16 egg yolks with a little milk and season. Pour this mixture through the neck of the bottle into the capon's skin and then sew up the neck, pushing it inside the bottle. Cork the bottle. Cook the bottle with capon in boiling water until the egg mixture grows and fills up the skin.
>
> The admiration of your guests is assured. They will not be able to imagine how the capon got inside the bottle with such a small neck.

POLISH ROAST CHICKEN
Pieczona Kura po Polsku

Chicken roasted in this way, and served with potatoes and cucumber (*mizeria*) salad (see page 108), is a classic national dish. Smoked chicken is also easy to buy and very popular. As a variation, chicken is sometimes eaten with an apple compote (see page 137).

Serves 4

1 x 1.6 kg (3¹/₂ lb) chicken with giblets
25 g (1 oz) butter

For the stuffing:
60 g (2¹/₄ oz) stale white bread
1 chicken liver
50 g (2 oz) butter
1 egg, separated
salt and pepper
2 teaspoons fresh chopped dill
2 sprigs parsley
scant 25 g (1 oz) dried breadcrumbs

Preheat the oven to 180C/350F/Gas 4. Prepare the chicken for cooking, rubbing butter on its skin and placing in a roasting dish.

To make the stuffing, soak the bread in warm water until soft, remove and squeeze out excess water. Put into a liquidiser with the liver and blend. Cream the butter, stir in the egg yolk and add the liver and bread. Mix well. Add salt, pepper, dill and parsley. Beat the egg white until stiff and fold in, together with the breadcrumbs.

Put the stuffing inside the chicken and sew up or secure by threading a toothpick across the hole. Cook in the oven for 20 minutes per lb and 20 minutes over, basting from time to time.

Serve with boiled potatoes and cucumber salad.

CHICKEN BADZIAK
Kura à la Badziak

Karolina Badziak, the mother-in-law of a Polish friend of mine, was born in Łask, a beautiful and ancient city in central Poland. Her love of cooking is coupled with a love of nature, and she is both a mushroom connoisseur and has a great understanding of herbs and their healing powers. Her married name, Badziak, originated from Budziak on the plains of Moldavia, once a frontier territory between the Polish Commonwealth and the Ottoman Empire.

Serves 4

1 x 1.6 kg (3^1/$_2$ lb) chicken with giblets
2 small onions, peeled and finely chopped
corn oil for frying
1 white bread roll
milk for soaking
4 tablespoons chopped fresh parsley
6 juniper berries
pinch tarragon
pinch marjoram
2-3 cloves garlic, crushed
salt and pepper
1 egg, beaten

For the stock:
2 carrots
handful parsley
2 sticks celery
1 bay leaf
5 peppercorns

Remove the giblets from the chicken and reserve them. Plunge the chicken into boiling water for 15 minutes to loosen its skin. Drain and carefully peel off the skin, trying to keep it in one piece. If this proves difficult, cut along the sides of the chicken and remove the two halves of skin from top and bottom.

Remove all the meat from the bones and put in a mincer with the giblets. Fry the onions in oil until golden. Soak the roll in milk until soft, squeeze out excess milk and add the bread – with the onion – to the chicken. Mince again. Pour the mixture into a large bowl and add the parsley, juniper berries, tarragon, marjoram, garlic, salt and pepper. Mix in the raw egg.

Spoon the chicken into its skin, either sewing up to form a whole – it should be shaped like a rugby ball – or wrapping in aluminium foil. The parcel should be watertight.

Place the chicken in a large saucepan with the carrots, parsley, celery, bay leaf and peppercorns, cover with water, bring to the boil and simmer for 1 hour.

Remove from the water and – removing the foil if used – place under a hot grill to brown the skin. Cut into slices and serve.

CHICKEN RISSOLES
Bitki z Kury

A similar recipe to this, but without the mushrooms and with a little paprika, appears in Edouard de Pomiane's *The Jews of Poland* (Pholiota Press Inc., California, 1985), a book of fascinating recollections and recipes from de Pomiane's travels in Poland in the 1920s.

Serves 4 (makes 16 rissoles)

....

> 2 chicken breasts, skin and bones removed
> 12 g (¹/₂ oz) butter
> 2 eggs, separated
> 2 slices white bread, soaked in milk
> salt and freshly ground black pepper
> 100 g (3¹/₂ oz) plain flour
> 1 large flat mushroom
>
> For frying:
> 1 egg
> 50 g (2 oz) dried breadcrumbs
> 75 g (2¹/₂ oz) butter

....

Preheat the oven to 220C/425F/Gas 7. Mince the chicken breasts finely. Cream the butter and egg yolks. Squeeze the bread as dry as possible and add. Stir in the chicken. Sift 75 g (2¹/₂ oz) of the flour into the chicken mixture and thoroughly mix to a non-sticky consistency that can be handled. Whisk the egg whites until stiff and fold in. Season. Wash or peel the mushroom and chop finely.

Sift the remaining flour on to a wooden or marble board. Form the chicken mixture into plum-sized balls, and into the middle of these push a little of the mushroom. Roll on the floured board to coat evenly.

Crack the egg into a bowl and whisk well. Sprinkle half the breadcrumbs on a large plate. Turn the floured balls in the egg and then in the breadcrumbs, using the remaining breadcrumbs as necessary. Set to one side.

Heat 50 g (2 oz) of butter into a large frying pan, and put in the chicken balls. You will probably need to do this in two batches. Fry until lightly browned all over. Lightly grease an ovenproof dish with the remaining butter, place the rissoles in this and when all are fried put into the hot oven for 10 minutes to ensure that they are cooked through. Serve with a mushroom or dill sauce (see pages 114 and 115).

Opposite: *Pierogi*

POLISH GOOSE
Gęś po Polsku

Serves 6

1 x 4.5 kg (10 lb) goose
salt
250 g (9 oz) vegetables, e.g. carrot, leek, parsnip,
    celery, parsley
50 g (2 oz) onion

For the sauce:
50 g (2 oz) butter or lard
50 g (2 oz) flour
salt
$1/4$ teaspoon grated nutmeg
1 apple, peeled, cored and diced
4 teaspoon marjoram
1-2 egg yolks

Remove the giblets from the goose and use to make goose giblet soup (see page 11). Immerse the goose in cold water and scrub thoroughly. Pat dry and rub with salt. With a sharp carving knife, split into two halves and put into a large pan. Pour boiling water over them to come half to three-quarters the way up and boil gently for 2 hours. Clean and prepare the vegetables and put them in the pan with the goose. Continue to boil gently for a further 30 minutes.

To make the sauce, melt the butter or lard, add the flour and allow to brown. Add enough stock from the goose to make a thin sauce, the consistency of single cream. Add salt to taste, and the nutmeg, apple and marjoram. Leave to simmer gently for about 10 minutes until the apple is soft. Divide the goose into portions and put it into the sauce. Bring to the boil just before serving and mix in the egg yolks.

Serve with pearl barley.

Opposite: Pidgeons Cooked Like Partridges (*Gołebie na Dziko*) and Red Cabbage (*Czerwona Kapusta*)

CASTELLAN'S TURKEY FILLET
Filety z Indyka po Kasztelańsku

It is thought that turkey first appeared on the Polish table in the early fifteenth century, because it was in those days that nobleman's sabres were first called turkeys, owing to their bent shape. Turkey has always been kept for special occasions, although it can be found in restaurants throughout the year. This recipe makes a good dinner party dish and, while last-minute cooking is unavoidable, much of the preparatory work such as stuffing the tomatoes and making the Béarnaise sauce can be done in advance. The finished dish is very pleasing, both to the eye and palate, with the natural dryness of the turkey blending beautifully with the rich Béarnaise sauce, and the tasty egg-and-vegetable tomatoes with their cheesy crust adding the finishing touch.

A grand-sounding recipe, it comes from Wierzyriek's restaurant in Cracow.

Serves 10

....

20 slices turkey breast
salt and pepper
25 g (1 oz) flour
75 g (2½ oz) lard
25g (1 oz) butter

For the stuffed tomatoes:
10 tomatoes
125 g (4½ oz) onion, peeled and finely chopped
100 g (3½ oz) butter
250 g (9 oz) cooked ham, chopped into strips
150 g (5 oz) flat mushrooms, chopped
2 hard-boiled eggs, diced
50 g (2 oz) peas
1 egg, beaten
100 g (3½ oz) Cheddar cheese

For the Béarnaise sauce:
2 small onions, peeled
3 sprigs tarragon
3 tablespoons tarragon vinegar
2 tablespoons malt vinegar
1 tablespoon water
2 egg yolks, beaten
50 g (2 oz) melted butter

To serve:
20 slices French bread
250 g (9 oz) button mushrooms
50 g (2 oz) butter

Take the turkey slices and beat each one out slightly on a board. Salt them and sprinkle some pepper and flour over them. Fry them in batches in hot lard, returning them to the pan and adding butter at the end to brown them.

Preheat the oven to 190C/375F/Gas 5. Halve the tomatoes, scoop out the insides and discard. Place the hollowed tomatoes on one side. To make the stuffing, fry the onion in the butter, add the ham, mushrooms, hard-boiled eggs and peas and fry for a few minutes. Remove from the heat, put in a bowl with the raw egg and mix. Spoon the stuffing into the empty tomatoes. Grate the cheese and sprinkle a little on top of each tomato. Bake in the oven for 15-20 minutes until crisp and bubbling.

To make the Béarnaise sauce, chop the onions and the tarragon leaves finely. Mix the vinegars and heat over a medium flame. Add the onion and tarragon leaves and cook for 2 minutes. When the vinegar has been reduced by half, add the water. In a bowl, pour the strained vinegar on to the beaten egg yolks. Set the bowl above a pan of boiling water and whisk constantly until the mixture has thickened. Take off the heat and gradually stir in the butter.

Toast the slices of French bread and fry the mushrooms in 50 g (2 oz) butter. Place a turkey fillet on each slice of bread, two to a plate. Decorate with Béarnaise sauce and mushrooms and put the stuffed tomatoes between each pair of turkey fillets. Serve at once.

MEAT AND OFFAL

During the sixteenth century, when Bona Sforza came to Poland from Italy to marry King Zygmunt, her Italian retinue was horrified by the Poles' heavy consumption of meat. In fact, the Papal *nuncio*, Ruggieri, while on a visit to Poland in 1569, stated that 'One Pole will eat as much meat as five Italians.'*

The majority of Poles still feel that a meal without meat is not a proper meal. Veal, beef and pork are the most popular meats although with the swing towards healthier eating the leaner game is much prized. Fish used to be kept for days in the religious calendar when meat is not allowed, but with the appearance of such things as "Fresh fish" counters in the new supermarkets fish is becoming an acceptable substitute for meat even when it is not a fast day.

Lamb is difficult to find in Poland. Whereas most countries celebrate Easter with a dish of lamb, in Poland a lamb appears on the table in sugar form, representing the "Lamb of God". Of the many veal, beef or pork dishes, recipes with beef are probably the most loved. Typical methods of cooking beef include placing bread stuffing between slices or rolls of beef, and braising the meat with a few vegetables and seasonings (often served for Sunday lunch with the stock from the beef kept for a tasty soup another day). For supper dishes meatballs and meat loaves are eaten. Marinades are very common – particularly with lamb or veal – and they certainly produce tender and succulent meat. Sauces for meat tend to be made by mixing a little sour cream and flour with the roasting juices or stock from the joint.

Offal, and in particular tripe (*flaczki*), has been popular for hundreds of years in Poland. Originally eaten by peasants in the country-side who learnt not to waste any part of their animals, tripe, knuckles, trotters, brains and innards soon all had a place in Polish cooking. Despite its humble origins, tripe was enjoyed by the Lithuanian King Jagiello and Polish Queen Jadwiga in the late fourteenth century. It remains in the forefront of Polish cooking and is considered a typical Polish dish.

*Maria Lemnis and Henryk Vitry, *Old Polish Traditions in the Kitchen and at the Table.*

ROAST BEEF À LA HUSSAR
Pieczeń Huzarska

Serves 6-8

1 kg (2¹/₄ lb) silverside
2 onions, peeled and thickly sliced
25 g (1 oz) butter
salt and pepper

For the stuffing:
25 g (1 oz) butter
3 tablespoons dried breadcrumbs
1-2 egg yolks
salt
2 tablespoons grated raw horseradish
  (not creamed or sauce)

Preheat the oven to 180C/350F/Gas 4. Season the meat, place in a roasting dish and roast for two hours, basting from time to time. Leave to cool.

Thoroughly mix the stuffing ingredients together. Slice the meat thinly, leaving alternate slices still attached to the base of the meat. Leave the sliced meat in place and put the filling between the slices all along the meat, securing with skewers or toothpicks. Return it to the roasting dish, adding the butter, onions, salt and pepper, and replace in the oven on the same heat for a further 20 minutes. To serve, remove the skewers or toothpicks and divide into portions, pouring a little of the roasting juices and the onions over each plate.

BEEF OLIVES
Zrazy

Mentioned first in the fourteenth century, *zrazy* are a traditional and ancient Polish dish, served with buckwheat or rice and beetroot purée (see page 98). Many types of *zrazy* exist, but the best ones are made from beef sirloin, as in this recipe.

Serves 6

....

1 small stale loaf of light rye bread, without seeds
4 medium-sized onions
25 g (1 oz) butter
salt and pepper
1 egg, beaten well
6 slices sirloin of beef
mustard
oil and butter for frying

....

Cut the crusts off the rye bread and soak in water until soft. Chop the onions and fry in the butter until lightly golden. Squeeze the excess water out of the bread and add the bread to the onions. Season well. Off the heat, mix in the beaten egg.

Beat out the sirloin slices thinly and season them. Spread each one thinly with mustard and pile one on top of the other. Leave for 15 minutes to absorb the mustard. Now spread the bread and onion filling thickly over each slice, 1 cm (½ in) high, leaving a space around the edges. Fold the sides into the middle and roll up. Secure with a toothpick.

Preheat the oven to 190C/375F/Gas 5. Heat the oil and a little butter in a large frying pan. Add the rolls – flap side down – and seal, turning to brown lightly all over. Put them in a casserole dish with enough water to come halfway up their sides, and cook in the oven for 1 hour.

BOILED BRISKET OF BEEF
Sztuka Mięsa

Served with hot horseradish sauce (see page 120), this dish is the Polish
equivalent to the English Sunday roast.

Serves 6

1.8 kg (4 lb) brisket of beef on the bone
2 onions
2 carrots
1 stick celery
2 bay leaves
pinch marjoram
pepper and salt

Put the meat into a flameproof casserole dish. Peel and chop the
onions, carrots and celery. Cover the meat with water and add the
vegetables and seasonings. Cover tightly and simmer for 3 hours. Remove
the meat from the pan and carve.

The strained stock can be drunk as a broth, to which you could
add liver dumplings or noodles, and this makes an excellent dish in
its own right.

BEEF À LA NELSON
Zrazy po Nelsońsku

Quite why this method of cooking beef is named after Nelson no one knows; perhaps it was his staple diet. Anyway, this recipe is now firmly embedded in the culinary traditions of Poland, and Nelson can be proud of it, since it is a wonderfully succulent dish.

Serves 6

....

> **6 slices, approximately 2.5 cm (1 in) thick, sirloin or tenderloin of beef**
> **salt and pepper**
> **25 g (1 oz) dried mushrooms, washed and soaked**
> **25 g (1 oz) onion, peeled**
> **25 g (1 oz) butter**
> **25 g (1 oz) flour**
> **200 ml (7 fl oz) single cream**
> **6 medium-sized potatoes**
> **50 g (2 oz) pork fat or lard for frying**

....

Season the meat and place on one side. Rinse the mushrooms in several changes of water, place in a small saucepan and cover with water. Leave for 30 minutes. Add the onion to the mushrooms and bring to the boil. When the mushrooms are soft, strain – reserving the stock and discarding the onion – and cut the mushrooms into narrow strips. Brown the butter slightly with the flour. Add some of the mushroom stock and the cream little by little, until you have a sauce with the consistency of double cream. Let it simmer for a few minutes, season and mix with the mushrooms.

Peel the potatoes, cut into segments as in an orange and boil them on a low heat until they are *just* done but still quite firm.

Melt the fat in a large flameproof casserole dish, put the slices of meat on the bottom side by side, and brown quickly on both sides. On each piece of beef place a portion of the cooked potatoes and pour the sauce on top. Bring to the boil and serve immediately, so that the meat is pink inside and juicy.

MEATBALLS WITH BUCKWHEAT
Zrazy z Kaszą Hreczaną

These meatballs can be flavoured with either mushrooms or tomato purée, depending on your preference; both go equally well with this recipe, but the addition of mushrooms makes a slightly richer dish.

Serves 4

$^1/_2$ medium-sized onion
25 g (1 oz) butter
450 g (1 lb) minced beef
salt and pepper
1 egg
2 tablespoons breadcrumbs
plain flour for coating
900 ml (1$^1/_2$ pints) beef stock
2 tablespoons flour
$^1/_2$ teaspoon salt
200 g (7 oz) flat mushrooms, chopped; or
   2 tablespoons concentrated tomato purée

For the buckwheat:
150 g (5 oz) buckwheat
1 tablespoon oil
salt
300 ml ($^1/_2$ pint) boiling water

Preheat the oven to 170C/325F/Gas 3. To make the meatballs, peel and chop the onion finely and fry lightly in the butter until golden brown. Put the meat in a bowl and season. Break in the whole egg, add the onion and mix well. Incorporate the breadcrumbs and work the mixture to a dough. Sprinkle flour onto a board, make about 12 ping-pong-sized balls from the meat and roll in flour to coat. Put the meatballs in a casserole dish, and pour over the beef stock to cover. Sprinkle on the flour and salt and mix. Add the chopped mushrooms, or the tomato purée. Cook in the oven for about 1 hour.

Half an hour before the meatballs are cooked, pour the buckwheat into a heavy saucepan. Pour the oil over it and 'dry' it on a gentle heat until it breaks and looks shiny, about 8-10 minutes. Cool, sprinkle with salt and cover with the boiling water. Cook slowly on a low heat for about 15 minutes. Loosen with a fork, leave covered for a few minutes and serve.

Pot Roast Beef
Sztufada

This needs to be started 48 hours in advance

Serves 4

....

1 kg (2¼ lb) sirloin of beef

For the marinade:
1 litre (1¾ pints) water
2-3 tablespoons red wine vinegar
1-2 onions, sliced
3 bay leaves
4-6 juniper berries

25 g (1 oz) lard
25 g (1 oz) butter
3 carrots
2 onions
1 stick celery
1 tablespoon parsley
2 cloves garlic
1 tablespoon dried mushrooms, washed and soaked
1 rasher smoked bacon, diced
2 beef stock cubes
2 litres (3½ pints) water
salt and pepper

....

Put the beef into a large pot, mix together the marinade ingredients and pour over the meat. Cover and leave in a cool place such as the larder or cool cupboard for 48 hours, turning from time to time.

Remove the beef from the marinade and pat dry. Make deep slits at random in the meat and fill them with slivers of lard. Melt the butter in a flameproof casserole, add the beef and seal all over.

Peel and chop the carrots and onions. Chop the celery and parsley. Crush the garlic. Add all these to the beef, together with the mushrooms and bacon. Dissolve the stock cubes in 2 litres (3½ pints) of boiling water and pour over the beef. Season well. Cover and leave to simmer slowly for approximately 2 hours.

Carve the beef into thin slices. Remove the vegetables from the stock and blend them with a little cream to serve as a sauce with the meat. The remaining stock makes an excellent broth.

MEAT LOAF STUFFED WITH EGGS
Klops

This dish is a good example of the many simple yet satisfying recipes in Polish cooking which, although still much eaten today, predate any sophisticating foreign influences.

Serves 4

2 eggs, hard-boiled
50 g (2 oz) stale bread
25 g (1 oz) onion
20 g (³/₄ oz) butter
500 g (1 lb 2 oz) beef, pork or a mixture, minced
1 egg, beaten
salt and pepper
25 g (1 oz) dried breadcrumbs
1 tablespoon chopped fresh parsley
50 g (2 oz) pork fat or lard for roasting

Peel the hard-boiled eggs and quarter them lengthways. Soak the stale bread in water, and when soft squeeze out the excess water and mince. Peel and chop the onion and fry in the butter until lightly golden. Mix the meat thoroughly with the bread, onion and beaten egg. Add salt and pepper and knead briefly.

Sprinkle the breadcrumbs on a large board and place the meat mixture on top fairly thinly in the form of a rectangle (roughly A4 size). Along one side, arrange the egg quarters, pointing them in towards the middle, and sprinkle them with parsley. Roll the meat up into a thick cylinder, starting from the side where the eggs are so that they will be in the middle.

Heat the oven to 220C/425F/Gas 7. Put the fat in a narrow and fairly deep baking tray. Place in the oven and let it melt. Add the meat loaf to it, basting thoroughly with the fat. Cover the tray with foil and bake in the oven for 1 hour 15 minutes, basting the meat frequently. Cut into slices and serve.

POLISH SAUSAGE IN TOMATO SAUCE
Kiełbasa w Sosie Pomidorowym

There are many types of Polish sausage, or *kiełbasa* as it is known, and they are much eaten in Poland as a snack with vodka, in soups, or in dishes in their own right, as here. The more well-known varieties such as *wiejska* (country sausage), *Krakowska* (garlic Cracow sausage) or *mysliwska* (hunter's sausage) can easily be found in delicatessen shops in England, as Polish sausage is exported all over the world. The very best sausages are those freshly made in the countryside. City dwellers can find them at specialist stalls in private markets. Any variety of Polish sausage will do for this dish.

Serves 2

50 g (2 oz) pork fat or lard
25 g (1 oz) onion, peeled and finely chopped
50 g (2 oz) flour
200 ml (7 fl oz) water or beef stock
1¹/₂ tablespoons tomato purée
pinch each sugar, salt and pepper
200 g (7 oz) Polish sausage (kiełbasa)

Melt the fat and brown it lightly with the onion. Add the flour and brown again. Gradually stir in the water or stock and bring to the boil. Add the tomato purée, salt and pepper, and sugar. Skin the sausage, cut it into big cubes, and add to the sauce. Simmer the sauce for a few more moments so that the flavours blend and the sausage is heated through.

Serve with potatoes or fried buckwheat.

THE KNIGHTS 1
Półmisek po Rycerski

Here is another dish from the Wierzynek Resta
bottled by Globus, is widely available in delicates

Serves 6

....

> 400 g (14 oz) fillet of pork
> 400 g (14 oz) fillet of veal
> 400 g (14 oz) pork joint or chops
> 600 g (1 lb 5 oz) large button mushrooms
> 180 g (6$^{1}/_{4}$ oz) butter
> 300 g (10$^{1}/_{2}$ oz) onions
> 652 g (1 lb 7 oz) jar of paprika (mild),
>   cut into tiny cubes
> 200 g (7 oz) Cheddar cheese

....

Cube all the meat into bite-sized pieces and fry in 100 g (3$^{1}/_{2}$ oz) of
the butter until well browned. Melt the remaining butter in a separate pan.
Wash the mushrooms lightly, peel and halve the onions and add both to the
butter. Cook until the onions are soft.

Arrange the meat on skewers, alternating it with mushrooms, onions
and paprika. To serve, lay the skewers on plates, grate the cheese and
sprinkle over.

STUFFED LAMB TROTTERS
Nóżki Baranie Nadziewane

This recipe is frorn the collection of Wojciech Wieladko, published in
Warsaw in 1800.

Cook lambs' trotters. Bone them. Lift the skin a little and stuff
them. Make the stuffing from lamb or veal meat mixed with:
słonina (pork fat), dripping; some beef; salt; pepper; herbs;
mushrooms. All this should be finely chopped and blended before
putting inside the trotters. Coat the trotters in beaten eggs and try
with słonina or butter. Serve garnished with parsley.

LEG OF VEAL
Noga Cielęca

allow 24 hours for the veal to marinate, the preparations for this dish should be started the day before it is to be eaten.

Serves 6

....

For the marinade:
1 bottle dry white wine
15 juniper berries
salt and pepper
2 bay leaves

1 kg (2¹/₄ lb) leg of veal
50 g (2 oz) butter for roasting
salt and pepper
50 g (2 oz) butter
1 heaped tablespoon flour
3 tablespoons sour cream

....

Prepare the marinade, mixing the ingredients as listed above. Put the veal in a pot and pour the marinade over. Leave for 24 hours in a larder or cool cupboard, turning from time to time.

Preheat the oven to 180C/350F/Gas 4. Remove the veal from the marinade and dry. Rub the meat with butter, season well and bake in the oven until nicely coloured – approximately 2 hours. When the veal is cooked, make a roux from the butter and flour and gradually stir in any juices from the veal. Add 125-250 ml (¹/₄-¹/₂ pint) of the strained marinade and lastly stir in the sour cream.

Carve the veal into slices, arrange on a deep plate and pour over the sauce.

VEAL CUTLETS À LA VIENNOISE
Sznycel po Wiedeńsku

This Austrian dish has been part of international cuisine for some time. It is particularly popular in Poland.

Serves 4

....

> 4 veal cutlets
> salt and pepper
> 50 g (2 oz) flour
> egg, beaten
> 50 g (2 oz) breadcrumbs
> 50 g (2 oz) butter

....

Pound the veal cutlets to make them thin and even. Season on both sides. Put the egg, flour and breadcrumbs on three separate plates. Coat each cutlet lightly in flour, dip into the egg and lastly coat in bread-crumbs, making sure they are well covered.

Melt a little butter in a large frying pan and fry the veal gently for 5-10 minutes, turning once, until golden on both sides. Serve.

Lamb, Polish Style
Baranina po Polsku

The lamb should be marinated for at least 24 hours before it is cooked. Flavoured with garlic, seasoned and then braised gently, this method makes a wonderfully moist dish full of flavour, and transforms the meat into something quite special.

Serves 6

For the marinade:
2 litres (3¹/₂ pints) water
300 ml (¹/₂ pint) malt vinegar
2 bay leaves
5 peppercorns

1.8 kg (4 lb) boned leg of lamb
4-5 cloves garlic
salt and pepper
oil for frying
1 bay leaf

For the sauce:
300 ml (¹/₂ pint) sour cream
3 tablespoons flour
salt and pepper

To make the marinade, put the water, vinegar, 2 bay leaves and the peppercorns in a large pan and bring to the boil. Put the lamb in a glass, Pyrex or china – but not aluminium – dish and pour over the boiling marinade to cover the lamb. Leave it in a cool cupboard or larder for up to two days and for at least 24 hours, turning occasionally.

Remove the lamb and dry with paper towels. Cut the garlic into fine slivers and make small slits in the lamb, tucking the garlic into them and also into the cavity where the bone was. Season the meat well.

Heat the oil in a deep pan, add the lamb and seal all over. Add water to come halfway up the sides of the lamb. Put in a bay leaf and simmer for 2 hours.

To make the sauce, mix the sour cream with the flour and heat very gently, without boiling (or the sour cream will curdle). Season with salt and pepper.

To serve, carve the lamb and hand the sauce around separately.

ROAST PORK WITH CARAWAY
Schab Wieprzowy po Polsku

Serves 6

....

1.8 kg (4 lb) loin of pork
2 teaspoons salt
teaspoon dried marjoram
1 heaped teaspoon caraway seeds
50 g (2 oz) pork fat or lard

....

Preheat the oven to 220C/425F/Gas 7. Score the fat of the pork with a sharp knife, and rub the salt, marjoram and caraway seeds over the meat. In a large pan, melt the pork fat and, over a high heat, seal the meat rapidly. When the pork is brown all over, put it into a roasting dish, and place in the oven. Roast for 2¹/₂ hours, basting frequently.

Serve with either sauerkraut, red cabbage, roasted buckwheat or *kopytka* (Little Hoofs; see page 91).

The best method for cooking meat
According to a recipe published in 1753:

You can use bison, moose, stag, wild goat or whatever. Divide it into pieces and put into a clay dish. Spread butter over the meat. Fry a lot of onion, apples and parsley and add to the meat. Season with salt and cook in stock. Half way through the cooking time add wine vinegar, slices of lemon, sultanas, pepper, cinnamon, cloves, nutmeg and cook for the remaining time needed.

BRAIN IN RAMEKINS
Móżdżek

Serves 2

....

250 ml (scant ¹/₂ pint) water
1 bay leaf
3 peppercorns
salt
dash vinegar
pinch parsley
400 g (14 oz) calf's brain (the butcher should have
    removed the membrane)
300 ml (¹/₂ pint) béchamel sauce (see page 124)
25 g (1 oz) Cheddar cheese, grated

To garnish:
1 tablespoon fresh breadcrumbs fried in
    25 g (1 oz) butter
slices of lemon

....

Preheat the oven to 190C/375F/Gas 5. Boil the water with the seasonings and add the brain. Simmer for 5 minutes, until it whitens. Strain and discard the seasonings. Cut the brain into cubes and mix with the béchamel sauce. Grease two ramekins and fill with the mixture, then sprinkle with grated cheese. Bake for 15 minutes.

Pour the browned breadcrumbs on top, and serve with slices of lemon.

BREADED PORK CHOPS
Kotlet Schabowy

Serves 4

---

4 medium-sized pork chops
salt and pepper
25 g (1 oz) plain flour
1 whole egg, beaten
25 g (1 oz) breadcrumbs
oil or lard for frying
25 g (1 oz) butter

Beat out the pork chops until they are fairly thin. Season with salt and pepper and set to one side. On separate plates pour the flour, egg and breadcrumbs. Dip each chop into the flour, coating it on both sides, and then dip into the beaten egg. Finally press the chops on to the breadcrumbs, turning once, and ensuring an even coating.

Heat sufficient oil or lard to come halfway up the chops in a large frying pan. When very hot add the pork and cook over a high flame for 5-6 minutes each side. Lower the heat, add the butter and cook for a few minutes more until nicely golden.

Ox Tongue in Polish Sauce
Ozór w Szarym Sosie

Serves 6

....

1 x 2 kg (4¹/₂ lb) fresh ox tongue
1 tablespoon salt
1 onion, peeled
1 carrot

For the sauce:
2 teaspoons sugar
50 g (2 oz) butter
50 g (2 oz) flour
1¹/₂ tablespoons vinegar
50 g (2 oz) raisins or sultanas
25 g (1 oz) almonds, blanched and sliced
juice and rind of 1 lemon
250 ml (scant ¹/₂ pint) white wine
1 tablespoon honey

....

Wash the tongue, salt it and put it into a pan of boiling water to cover, together with the onion and carrot. Cover and simmer for 3-3¹/₂ hours, until soft. This can be tested by inserting a knife or skewer into the tongue. Take it out, reserving the water in which it was boiled, and remove the skin and gristle.

To make the sauce, melt the sugar in a small saucepan until lightly coloured. In another pan, make a roux with the butter and flour – allowing the flour to brown well – and add the sugar. Cook gently for 5 minutes. Gradually stir in approximately 500 ml (scant 1 pint) of the water in which the tongue was boiled, and add the vinegar. Bring to the boil and simmer for 5 minutes. Slice the tongue and put into a saucepan with the sauce. Add all the other ingredients and simmer for 15 minutes. Serve.

TRIPE
Flaczki

Serves 4

....

1 kg (2¹/₄ lb) beef tripe
salt
1.5 litres (3 pints) beef stock
pinch of marjoram
pinch of paprika
50 g (2 oz) butter
1 tablespoon flour

To garnish:
25 g (1 oz) breadcrumbs
25 g (1 oz) grated cheese
1 tablespoon chopped parsley

....

Clean the tripe carefully and rinse in warm water several times. Add to a pan of salted boiling water and simmer until tender but not soft (3¹/₂ hours). Drain the tripe and rinse thoroughly. Cut it into narrow strips. Bring the stock to the boil and add the tripe. Stir in marjoram and paprika and cook until the tripe is soft enough to be crushed between the fingers – about 45 minutes.

Melt half the butter, add the flour and cook until golden brown. Gradually stir in a little stock from the tripe to make a sauce with the consistency of double cream and bring to the boil, mixing constantly. Remove the tripe and vegetables from the stock and mix with the sauce.

Arrange the tripe on a plate. Melt the remaining butter and brown the breadcrumbs in it. Pour over the tripe. Sprinkle on the grated cheese and parsley. Serve with suet dumplings (see page 26).

GAME

Game has always been abundant in the forests of Poland, and for this reason formed an important part of the Polish diet. Today, all over Europe, big game such as wild boar or deer is more common than ever, while birds like partridges and pheasants are on the decrease. Game can be bought relatively easily in the countryside, but tends to be difficult to find elsewhere.

Partridge, pheasant, wild duck, quail, hare and wild boar are the most popular, while ancient delicacies such as elk nostrils and bear paws in honey are now mostly confined to culinary history rather than seen on the dining table.

Poland, like Hungary, organises shoots for foreigners, and many try the challenge of shooting wild boar. In the old days the wild boar were tracked down on horseback and killed with bows and arrows, spears or knives. These, however, were soon replaced by firearms, and the wild boar would then be tracked on foot, using dogs and beaters. One exception to this was a cousin, Justyna Wolańska, who in the early nineteenth century, perhaps uniquely, still hunted wild boar on horseback with a spear in the forests of her estate, Czarnokońce in south-eastern Poland.

My father, who shot wild boar before the Second World War in the approaches to Poland's Carpathian Mountains, particularly recalls the late summer shoots, which took place at night. On these occasions the boar would be watched and followed in the moonlight as it came out to eat rye, wheat or potatoes in the nearby fields. Because of the damage inflicted on the crops by these animals, peasants would take it in turn to stand guard over their plots, raising the alarm if a boar came too close. To while away the time they would sing, and the still night would carry snatches of their song far afield. To my father, the haunting melodies of these peasant airs have become inextricably entwined with his childhood memories of those clear early autumn nights spent on his father's estate of Koropiec.

Wild boar, unlike other game, is shot all year round; only the female has a closed season during breeding. In winter, shooting of boar and other game often takes place in temperatures of well below freezing, and consequently a warming and nourishing lunch is served. Barley soup (*krupnik*), vodka and Hunter's Stew (*bigos*) are typical of what is eaten around a large fire in the forest before the shooting continues.

Poles prepare game in a variety of ways for the table. The larger animals such as wild boar or venison, unless very young, are normally marinated to tenderise the meat. The favourite seasoning with all game is dried juniper berries; not many of which are needed to provide a strong flavour. These are cooked with the game, or added to the marinade, or used to make juniper sauce, which is then served as a gravy. Alternatively, if the game is roasted, sour cream is added to the roasting juices and this is then handed round with the meat. Rosehip sauce is another traditional accompaniment to game, and garlic another favourite seasoning. Beetroot or red cabbage are the normal side dishes.

Game has always been popular in Polish cuisine and it is interesting to see how it was cooked over the centuries. Here are a few choice recipes from *The Well Prepared Cook* by Jan Szyttler, published in 1830.

SNOW PARTRIDGES
Białe Kuropatwy

Beat 16 egg whites and put on a large serving dish, covering the sides only and leaving the middle empty. Place unplucked partridge heads and necks in it so that they are well visible. Put the dish in the oven and bake dry.

Separately bake the partridge meat and then place in the middle of the dish, pouring over it any juices from the cooking. Garnish with mushrooms and truffles and serve at once.

PARTRIDGES WITH ANCHOVY BUTTER
Kuropatwa w Cieśie

Bake partridges and when ready put on a serving dish. Make slits in the meat and fill them with anchovy butter. Pour a good sauce over and decorate with lemon slices.

QUAIL IN PÂTE
Przepiórki w Cieście

Pluck and clean quails, then bone them. Dissolve 100 g (3¹/₂ oz) of butter in a frying pan, add parsley, mushrooms and lemon juice. Add the quail meat and cook for a few minutes. When it becomes white put each quail on a round of puff pastry and cover with another round. The top pastry round should have a hole in the middle. Brush with egg and bake. When ready, put some good sauce into each hole and garnish.

HARE BAKED WITH SAUSAGES
Pieczony Zając z Kielbaskami

When the hare is cleaned, bone it and finely chop the meat. Add to it 450 g (1 lb) of *słonina* (pork fat); 2 finely chopped bread rolls – soaked in milk beforehand – scrambled egg from 8 eggs; nutmeg; pepper and 225 g (¹/₂ lb) butter. Pound it all well and mix together. Add 12 raw egg yolks and pass it all through a sieve. Beat the 12 egg whites and fold into the meat, then put all of it in a pâté dish, which should be brushed with butter and lined with slices of sausage. This should be cooked in another pan with water coming halfway up the hare dish. Cover and cook for 1¹/₂ hours. Serve with sauce.

HARE BRAISED IN WINE
Duszony Zając w Winie

To allow sufficient time for the hare to marinate, preparations for this dish must be started 2-3 days before it is to be eaten.

Serves 8

For the marinade:
500 ml (scant 1 pint) water
100 g (3^1/$_2$ oz) onion, peeled and chopped
1 bay leaf
6 juniper berries
6 peppercorns
pinch of allspice
250 ml (scant ^{1}/$_2$ pint) vinegar

2-2.3 kg (4^1/$_2$-5 lb) saddle and hind of hare
100 g (3^1/$_2$ oz) lard
150 g (5 oz) smoked bacon, thinly sliced
150 g (5 oz) onion, peeled and sliced
25 g (1 oz) breadcrumbs
1 small teaspoon paprika
salt
250 ml (scant ^{1}/$_2$ pint) red wine

To make the marinade, boil the water with the onion and seasonings. Leave to cool. Mix it with the vinegar. Put the hare in a non-aluminium dish, pour the marinade over and leave it in a cool cupboard or larder for 2 to 3 days, turning every day. Take out the meat and rinse once. Pat dry. Cover with lard.

Put half the bacon slices on the bottom of a wide flameproof casserole dish. Cut the hare into pieces and place on top. Add the onion, then the breadcrumbs mixed with paprika. Add salt. Cover with the remaining bacon slices. Pour 125 ml (1 pint) of the marinade over the bacon, plus 120 ml (1 pint) of water and the red wine. Braise, covered, for 2^1/$_2$-3 hours.

Serve with potatoes and red cabbage.

POLISH HARE IN CREAM
Zając ze Śmietaną

To allow sufficient time for the hare to marinate, preparations for this dish must commence 2-3 days before it is to be eaten. This recipe is typically Polish, with its flavouring of sour cream and the use of caramel to colour the sauce.

Serves 4

For the marinade:
500 ml (scant 1 pint) water
100 g (3¹/₂ oz) onion, peeled and sliced
pinch of allspice
6 peppercorns
6 juniper berries
250 ml (scant ¹/₂ pint) vinegar

saddle and hind of hare
100 g (3¹/₂ oz) bacon fat
salt
50 g (2 oz) fat
50 g (2 oz) flour
250 ml (scant ¹/₂ pint) sour cream
caramel for colouring (see page 123),
    made with 150 g (5 oz) granulated
    sugar and 75 ml (2¹/₂ fl oz) water

Make the marinade as described on page 80. Put the hare in a non-aluminium dish. Pour the marinade over the hare and leave for 2-3 days in a cool cupboard or larder, turning every day.

Preheat the oven to 190C/375F/Gas 5. Remove the hare, rinse and pat dry. Lard it with bacon fat and salt it. Melt the fat in a frying pan and seal the hare quickly on all sides. Place in a roasting dish with a little water, and put in the oven for 2 hours, basting often.

When tender, remove from the oven and cut into pieces. Add the flour to the juices in the roasting dish, place on the hob, bring up to the boil and, off the heat, stir in the sour cream. Make the caramel according to the recipe on page 123, and pour into the sauce.

Arrange the hare on a plate and pour over the sauce. Serve.

MARINATED AND ROAST WILD BOAR
Marynowany i Pieczony Dzik

This needs to be prepared 1-2 days in advance.

Serves 8

....

2 kg (4¹/₂ lb) piece wild boar meat (from the rump)

For the marinade:
2 onions, peeled and chopped
6 peppercorns
salt
2 carrots, chopped
600 ml (1 pint) red wine
100 g (3¹/₂ oz) lard
100 g (3¹/₂ oz) butter
salt
¹/₂ teaspoon paprika

For the sauce:
150 ml (1 pint) red wine
50 g (2 oz) tomato purée
2 cloves garlic, crushed
salt and pepper
4 tablespoons single cream

....

Rinse and dry the meat and remove the outer membrane. Rub the meat with the onions, peppercorns and salt. Put in a dish, add the carrots and pour over the red wine. Leave in a cold place such as a larder or refrigerator for 1 to 2 days, turning over from time to time.

Preheat the oven to 180C/350F/Gas 4. Cut the lard into thick chunks. Take the meat out of the marinade, reserving the vegetables, and lard it irregularly, putting the lard in very deep with a larding needle. Heat the butter in a pan and brown the wild boar on all sides.

Put the meat in an ovenproof dish, add the butter it was fried in, the vegetables from the marinade, salt and paprika. Sprinkle with water, cover and bake slowly until tender, about 2 hours, basting frequently.

Take the meat out when cooked and cut across the fibres at a slight angle, cutting slices 1 cm (¹/₂ in) thick. Do not mix their sequence but put back into the dish. In a separate pan bring to the boil all the ingredients for the sauce. Allow to bubble for a few minutes and then pour over the meat. Serve with spooned dumplings (*kładzione kluski*) (see page 91).

WILD BOAR CUTLETS
Kotlety z Dzika

The meat for this dish must be tender but does not need to be marinated.

Serves 4

1 kg (2¹/₄ 1b) tender meat from a young boar
50 g (2 oz) flour
2 eggs, beaten
100 g (3¹/₂ oz) breadcrumbs
100 g (3¹/₂ oz) fat for frying

Cut the meat into slices and beat out until thin. Turn in the flour, dip into the egg and then coat well with breadcrumbs. Melt the fat in a large frying pan and when hot fry the slices until well cooked on either side.

These can be served with horseradish sauce (see page 120).

PIGEONS COOKED LIKE PARTRIDGES
Gołębie na Dziko

The richness of the pigeon blends well with the full-bodied taste of juniper, the seasoning most commonly used with game. Indigenous to the country, the wood of the juniper tree is also used to smoke hams and *poledwica* (the finest Polish cured ham).

Serves 4

4 young pigeons
40 g (1½ oz) juniper berries
50 g (2 oz) butter
salt
50 g (2 oz) pork fat or butter
2 tablespoons water
2 tablespoons white wine or cider
4 rounds of toast

Clean the pigeons and put on one side. In a pestle and mortar crush the juniper berries. Cream the butter and pound to a paste with the juniper berries. Rub the mixture inside and outside the pigeons and leave for 4 hours.

Salt the inside and outside of the pigeons before cooking, and put 6 g (1 oz) more fat or butter into each bird. With the remaining butter seal the birds quickly over a high heat. Put in a flameproof casserole, adding the water and white wine or cider. Braise for 30-45 minutes. Divide the birds in half, cutting along their breast bone with a sharp knife, and place on top of rounds of toast. Cover with the juices from the pan and serve.

WILD DUCK IN MUSHROOM SAUCE
Dzika Kaczka w Sosie Grzybowym

Wild duck are only available during the shooting season from 1 September until 28 February. They are at their best in November and December and are easily bought from any butcher dealing in game. Unlike the domestic duck, they are lean birds and have a gamey taste.

Serves 4

2 wild duck
50 g (2 oz) butter
1 onion, peeled and chopped
25 g (1 oz) dried mushrooms
salt and pepper
25 g (1 oz) pearl barley
3 tablespoons sour cream
3 tablespoons flour

Clean the duck, melt the butter and add the duck to it, browning quickly all over. Add the onion to the duck. Rinse the mushrooms in several changes of water and leave to soak for 30 minutes. Cook in the water they were soaked in until soft, then pour the mushrooms and their cooking water over the duck – it should come halfway up the sides of the ducks. Season, and cook over a medium heat for about an hour.

Meanwhile, cover the pearl barley with a little cold water, bring to the boil and simmer for about an hour.

Remove the duck from the pan. Mix the sour cream with the flour and stir into the pot. Strain the sauce, chop the mushrooms finely and return them to the sauce. Simmer for a few minutes.

Carve the duck and arrange on a suitable plate. Drain the pearl barley and spoon on to the plate with the duck. Pour the sauce over and serve at once.

PARTRIDGE FRICASSÉE
Kuropatwa Fricassée

This is an extremely easy and very tasty dish.

Serves 4

....

> 4 partridges
> 8 slices bacon
> 100 g (3½ oz) butter
> 6 juniper berries
> 1 tablespoon water
> 150 ml (¼ pint) single cream
> 1 tablespoon lemon juice
> 1 tablespoon breadcrumbs
> salt and pepper

....

Preheat the oven to 220C/425F/Gas 7. Clean the partridges and cover their breasts with the bacon. Roast for 20 minutes until they are halfcooked. Melt the butter in a flameproof casserole dish, set aside the bacon and keep warm, split the partridges in half along their breastbone with a sharp knife, and put into the dish. Add the juices from the roasting pan, the juniper berries and 1 tablespoon water. Allow to bubble for 10 minutes and then add the cream, lemon juice and breadcrumbs. Season and serve with the bacon.

PARTRIDGES WITH RED CABBAGE
Kuropatwa z Czerwoną Kapustą

In the south of Poland, where because of the warmer climate vineyards flourish, partridges are sometimes cooked wrapped in vine leaves. For the rest of Poland the following method is probably the most usual way of preparing them.

Serves 4

1 large red cabbage, coarsely chopped
1 onion, peeled and chopped
salt and pepper
250 g (9 oz) lard
150 ml (1 pint) red wine
4 partridges, rubbed with a little butter for roasting

Mix together the red cabbage, onion and some salt, and leave for one hour. Thoroughly drain off any water.

Preheat the oven to 220C/425F/Gas 7. In a large pot, pour boiling water on to the lard and melt over a medium flame. Add the cabbage and onion, and pour on the red wine. Season and mix well.

Put the partridges in a roasting tin and roast for 15-20 minutes until they are half-done. Remove from the oven. Remove half the cabbage mixture from the pot and put in the partridges, cut in half, putting the rest of the cabbage back on top. Pour the juices from the roasting tin into the pan and braise, covered, until all is soft (about an hour). Serve.

VEGETABLES AND SIDE DISHES

Poland means 'field country', and the produce from the fields, such as rye, wheat, millet, barley and buckwheat, is eaten widely, far more than either vegetables or salads. These cereals (*kasza*) are used in soups, as a stuffing for meat or cabbage, or simply fried or baked and served as a side dish. In pagan times gifts of cereals, honey and cheese were offered to the goddesses of birth upon the arrival of a baby to ensure a long and successful life for the newborn child. Of all the cereals grown in Poland, buckwheat is considered the finest.

The vegetables grown in Poland are those that can withstand the cold Polish winters and which are most suitable for storing, pickling or preserving. Even though greenhouses and market gardens thrive in Poland today, they have done little to change the basic pattern of vegetables used in the Polish kitchen, and concentrate more on growing flowers and fruits.

Potatoes are eaten as an alternative to cereals, and although they are popular, they have never posed a serious threat to the pre-eminent position of the indigenous grains. Potatoes and grains are considered as part of, rather than an accompaniment to, the main course. Potatoes are often used as dishes in their own right – in potato pancakes or potato and vegetable gratin, for example – and as an accompaniment to meat or fish, when they sometimes take the form of noodles, known as *kopytka* (meaning little hoofs, which they resemble), or they may be simply boiled and sprinkled with a little dill. Another side dish typical in this part of the world is dumplings, which are normally served with meat and stews.

Also from the fields come beetroot, another invaluable vegetable which can be stored during the winter. From beetroot are made the famous soup *barszcz* (see pages 164 and 184) and the equally ancient salad *ćwikła* (see page 111). They are served in many other forms, too: braised, puréed, baked, and even in a sweet dish, Beetroot Fried in Batter (see page 97), which contrasts well with game.

A less versatile food but one with an essential place on the Polish table is cabbage. White cabbage is pickled for sauerkraut, which is then used as a vegetable or a filling for *pierogi* (the Polish equivalent to ravioli). It also forms the basis of *bigos*, or Hunter's Stew (see page 165) and is also sometimes served as a salad, sprinkled with a little sugar and mixed with diced apples, onions and carrots. Red cabbage is eaten as a winter salad or with game, as in Partridges with Red Cabbage (see page 87), or simply cooked with a few sweet spices and served as a side dish.

From the forest come mushrooms, one of the most popular of all Polish foods. Endless culinary possibilities exist with a few fresh or dried mushrooms, and they are often used as a meat substitute on fast days.

BAKED BUCKWHEAT
Kasza Gryczana

Buckwheat is eaten in Poland in much the same way as rice is in England, except that it is not served with fish. It is a classic accompaniment to Beef Olives, Beef à la Nelson and meatballs. Buckwheat grains are available at any Polish delicatessen and many health food shops.

Serves 4

225 g (8 oz) buckwheat groats
500 ml (scant 1 pint) water
1 teaspoon salt
butter

Heat the oven to 150C/300F/Gas 2. Bring the water to the boil and add the salt and buckwheat. Simmer for 5 minutes, stirring from time to time. Drain well. Arrange in an ovenproof dish and bake in a low oven for 20-30 minutes until all the grains are dry and cooked. Put a knob of butter in the dish and serve.

Mamaliga
Mamałyga

Similar to the Italian polenta, this is a Romanian dish, which has penetrated into south-eastern Poland, although it remains unknown elsewhere in the country. My father, who comes from the south-east, recalls that in autumn after the corn was harvested, bundles of it were plaited and hung in long strips on the right and left of cottage doorways where it remained until needed, adding much colour to the village meanwhile. It was from these golden decorations that the corn groats were made and then *mamałyga*.

Serves 4

1 litre (1³/4 pints) water
pinch of salt
225 g (8 oz) corn groats
50 g (2 oz) butter
50 g (2 oz) Gruyère cheese

Bring the water to the boil, add the salt and sift in the corn groats. Simmer for 15 minutes, stirring all the time. Heat the oven to 170C/325F/Gas 3. Grease an ovenproof dish with half the butter and fill with alternate layers of corn groats and finely grated cheese, finishing with a layer of cheese. Dot with the remaining butter and bake in the oven until golden brown.

SPOONED DUMPLINGS
Kładzione Kluski

These are best served with a stew.

Serves 6

1 egg
pinch of salt
200 ml (7 fl oz) milk
200 g (7 oz) plain flour
butter

Beat the egg in a small bowl. Add salt and a little of the milk, mixing well. Stir in some flour. Gradually alternating milk and flour, add both to the bowl until you have a soft dough.

Bring some water to the boil, add a pinch of salt and drop teaspoons of the dough into it. Let the dumplings rise to the surface and leave them to cook for about 3 minutes.

Melt a little butter. Remove the dumplings from the water, pour a little melted butter over them to prevent them sticking together and serve.

LITTLE HOOFS
Kopytka

These noodles, which are a good accompaniment to any meat dish, look like little hoofs, hence the name.

Serves 6

4 or 5 potatoes, cooked and mashed
1 egg
flour

Mix the potatoes with the egg and add flour until you have a loose dough that does not stick to your fingers. Roll out the dough on a floured board and cut into thin noodles. Bring some salted water to the boil and drop the noodles into it, making sure they do not stick to the bottom. They are ready when they float to the surface.

ONION FLAN
Placek Cebulowy

This is a rich and deliciously creamy flan with a strong onion flavour.

Serves 6-8

For the pastry:
250 g (9 oz) flour
pinch of salt
125 g (4¹/₂ oz) butter
1 egg
beans, for baking blind

For the filling:
500 g (1 lb 2 oz) onions
125 g (4¹/₂ oz) butter
250 ml (scant ¹/₂ pint) sour cream
4 eggs
300 g (10¹/₂ oz) Cheddar cheese, grated
salt and pepper

Make the pastry first. Sift the flour into a bowl, add the salt and make a well in the middle. Add the butter, cut into small pieces, and the egg. Work with your fingertips into a light, crumbly mixture and then knead into a dough. Wrap in clingfilm and chill in the refrigerator for 20-30 minutes. Heat the oven to 200C/400F/Gas 6. Roll out the dough on a floured board. Grease a 26 cm (12 in) flan dish and line with the pastry. Prick the pastry all over with a fork, line with greaseproof paper and fill with baking beans. Put in the oven for 20 minutes. Remove the beans and the paper and return the pastry case to the oven for 5 minutes so that it can dry out, then remove it from the oven.

Meanwhile, make the filling. Chop the onions finely and fry in the butter until lightly browned. Whisk the sour cream with the eggs very thoroughly, and stir in the onions and cheese, adding salt and pepper to taste.

Pour the filling into the cooked pastry, return to the oven and bake at the same temperature for approximately 1 hour or until firm and nicely browned on top.

Serve hot with a dry white wine.

MUSHROOMS

Mushrooms are eaten in large quantities in Poland, and mushroom picking is part of everyone's life. Popular in many forms, they are used as a meat replacement in Lent and on other fast days. Certainly mushrooms will appear without fail – in one form or another – at the great meal on Christmas Eve, as this is a meatless day. Dried mushrooms are used extensively to flavour soups and sauces. In Warsaw, in the old town, there is often a wonderful smell of cooked mushrooms pervading the cobbled streets, as mushroom *bułki* (rolls) – equivalent to our hot dogs – are sold at the windows of one or two cafés.

I have read that there are thirty-one different varieties of mushrooms approved by the Ministry of Health and Social Welfare in Poland, and many more unapproved ones. Of these the better known are the *rydz* or saffron milk cup, with pink and green rings on its head, delicious fried with a little sour cream; the *borowik* or *Boletus edulis* which is dried and exported to England and elsewhere in large quantities; the *kurka* or chanterelle, which can also be dried and is perhaps the mushroom most commonly used in French cooking; *pieczarki*, the ordinary field mushroom; and *smardze* or the morel. There are others too, with such evocative names as *maślak* or the willowy, mottled *czubajka*; the golden or grey *gaska*, the *kozlarz babka* and the *podgrzybek*, which literally means 'the little under mushroom'.

Obviously, despite the modern hazards of pollution, not much has changed since Mickiewicz wrote about mushroom gathering in *Pan Tadeusz*, his tale of the gentry in 1811 and 1812:

Mushrooms were plentiful: the boys preferred
The *vixens* (that's the Lithuanian word)
Emblems of maidenhood; uneat by worms,
No insect ever light upon their forms.
The girls the slender *forester* pursued,
In song called colonel of the mushroom brood.
All sought the orange agaric, less tall
And famed in song, but tastiest of all,
Or salt or fresh, and good in any season.
The Seneschal picked flybane – for a reason.
The other kinds of mushrooms are not favoured.
Because they're harmful or are evil flavoured.
They are not useless but for beasts are good,
Shelter the insects and adorn the wood.
They stand upon the grassy cloth in order
Like rows of plates: such as with scalloped border
The small *leaf mushrooms*, silver, red and gold
Like goblets that all kinds of liquor hold;

The *kids* like swelling cups turned upside down;
The *funnels* slim like champagne glasses grown;
The kind called *white* that broad and flattish gleam
Like china coffee cups filled full of cream;
The *puff-ball*, like a pepper pot, with black
Dust filled. The others all distinction lack,
Save by the wolves and hares unrecognised,
By human kind untold and unbaptised.

Dried Mushrooms and How to Use Them

The dried mushrooms found in the shops in Britain are the *Boletus edulis*, known in Poland as *borowik*, which derives from *bór*, meaning forest. This type of mushroom can be found growing in England, but since mushroom picking is not something the British have ever been interested in it goes unnoticed, and only the cultivated varieties are sold fresh. The boletus has a strong and earthy flavour and can be found in late summer and autumn in woods all over Europe. In England, both Italian and Polish delicatessens sell the dried boletus and, although expensive, it is a very worthwhile ingredient to have in your larder as the flavour it bestows on sauces and soups is quite superb, and it will keep for over a year.

Dried mushrooms must always be thoroughly rinsed in several changes of water, to remove the inevitable particles of earth, and they should then be soaked for 15-30 minutes until soft. They can either be cooked or added to cream, stock or other liquid to flavour it according to the recipe.

To Dry Mushrooms

Flat cap or field mushrooms are the most suitable for drying. Pick them fresh and trim off any ragged edges. With a damp cloth, gently wipe clean, and pull off the stalks. Thread string through a large needle and push it through the centre of each mushroom, tying a large knot for each mushroom to sit on, to prevent them touching each other (like knotted pearls). Hang in a warm place where air circulates for a few days until they have dried out. Cut the strings down and store the mushrooms in airtight jars.

MUSHROOMS WITH SOUR CREAM
Pieczarki w Śmietanie

Serves 4

50 g (2 oz) butter
1 medium onion, peeled and diced
2 cloves garlic, crushed
225 g (8 oz) flat mushrooms, sliced
salt and pepper
sour cream – quantity according to taste

Melt the butter in a frying pan and add the onion and garlic. Cook until golden. Add the mushrooms, cover and leave on a low heat to simmer. When the mushrooms are cooked, season them and pour over some sour cream. Serve.

MUSHROOM CUTLETS
Kotlety z Pieczarek

Serves 4

225 g (8 oz) flat mushrooms
3 tablespoons cooked rice
1 medium onion, peeled and diced
25 g (1 oz) butter
4 tablespoons parsley
salt and pepper
2 eggs, beaten separately
dried breadcrumbs for coating butter or oil for frying

Chop the mushrooms very finely and mix with the rice. Fry the onion in butter until golden. Chop the parsley. Mix all together, season, and add 1 egg to bind. Form into cutlets. Dip the cutlets into the remaining egg, press into breadcrumbs and fry in hot butter or oil until golden on both sides. Drain on kitchen towels.

Mushrooms Fried in Breadcrumbs
Pieczarki Panierowane

Serve these with tartare sauce (see page 122).

Serves 4

....

12 large flat mushrooms
flour for coating
.   **2 eggs, beaten**
dried breadcrumbs for coating
butter or oil for frying

....

Wipe the mushrooms clean and remove the stalks. Put a little flour, the eggs, and some breadcrumbs in three separate dishes. Dip the mushrooms first in the flour, then turn thoroughly in the egg and coat well with breadcrumbs.

Heat the butter or oil in a large frying pan and when hot add the mushrooms, frying on all sides. Remove from the pan and place gently on some kitchen towel for a few seconds, to remove the grease.

BEETROOT

To many people, beetroot is synonymous with Polish cooking, although, while it is certainly eaten and beetroot soups are popular, the Poles do not live off it. When eaten as a vegetable, beetroot is served in several different ways. Below are a few examples.

BEETROOT FRIED IN BATTER
Buraczki w Cieście

This goes well with all game dishes.

Serves 4

8 cooked baby beetroot
500 ml (scant 1 pint) single cream
5 egg yolks
2 heaped tablespoons flour
pinch of salt
$^1/_2$ level teaspoon sugar
8 cloves, crushed
3 tablespoons red wine
butter for frying
sugar

Peel the beetroot and cut into thick slices. To make the batter, beat the cream and egg yolks together in a pan over a gentle heat. Sprinkle in the flour, stirring all the time and leaving on the heat until it thickens. Remove and leave to cool.

Add the seasonings and wine. Dip the beetroot slices into the batter and fry in butter until golden on both sides. Serve sprinkled with sugar. The beetroot should be sweet and tender.

BRAISED BEETROOT
Buraczki

Serve with hare, duck, roast veal, beef, lamb, venison or wild boar.

Serves 6

> 3 medium-sized cooked beetroots
> 50 g (2 oz) lard for frying
> 2 tablespoons flour
> 150 ml (³/₄ pint) single cream
> dash of red wine vinegar
> salt and sugar to taste

Peel the beetroot and dice or grate them. Melt the lard and when hot add the beetroot. Mix well for a few minutes. Sprinkle the flour over the beetroot and add the cream. Mix well. Add the vinegar and salt and sugar to taste, mix again and leave to cook on a low heat (beetroot burns easily) for 10 minutes.

PURÉE OF BEETROOT
Buraczki

Serves 4

> 400 g (14 oz) cooked beetroot
> 40 g (1¹/₂ oz) butter
> 2 level tablespoons flour
> 300 ml (¹/₂ pint) milk
> 1 tablespoon sour cream
> squeeze of lemon juice
> salt and pepper
> sugar to taste

Chop the beetroot and purée coarsely. Melt the butter, stir in the flour and gradually add the milk, mixing constantly over a low heat. To this add the beetroot, the sour cream and a squeeze of lemon juice. Season with salt, pepper and sugar. Serve piping hot.

CABBAGE

CABBAGE PIE
Tort z Kapusty

Within the crisp yeast pastry of this pie lie layers of mushroom and eggs, cabbage and onion, making an unusual filling and very tasty luncheon dish. It can be served hot or cold but is more suitable hot as it is an ideal dish for winter days.

Serves 8

For the pastry:
125 g (4½ oz) butter
pinch of salt
500 ml (scant 1 pint) milk
50 g (2 oz) fresh yeast or 25 g (1 oz) dried yeast
600 g (1 lb 5 oz) flour
2 egg yolks

oil for cooking

For the stuffing:
250 g (9 oz) white cabbage
½ level teaspoon salt
25 g (1 oz) pork fat or lard
2 small onions, peeled and chopped
handful of dried mushrooms
2 egg whites
1 egg

To make the pastry, melt the butter, with the salt, in a small pan. When completely melted add most of the milk, reserving 55 ml, (2 fl. oz). Warm the reserved milk, crumble the yeast into it, and add a tiny amount of flour. Mix and leave in a warm place for about 15 minutes to rise. Sift the rest of the flour into a large bowl and add the butter and milk mixture. Add the egg yolks and mix well together. Add the frothy yeast mixture to the dough, mix again and leave to rise in a warm place for 1 hour.

To make the stuffing, finely slice the cabbage and sprinkle with salt. Leave for 30 minutes and press out any juices. Rinse well. Put the cabbage in a saucepan and add the fat and the chopped onion. Fry on a low heat.

Rinse the mushrooms in several changes of water, and leave to soak for 15 minutes. Cook in a little water until soft. Divide into two equal portions. Cut one portion very thinly, the other very thickly. Fry the egg whites in a pan as you would make a normal fried egg, and hard-boil the other egg, cutting it into pieces.

Preheat the oven to 200C/400F/Gas 6. When the dough has risen, smear a baking tray with oil and place half the dough, rolled out, on it. Spoon on all the stuffing – the cabbage, mushrooms, egg whites and egg in layers. Roll out the second half of the dough and cover the stuffing with it, pressing the edges of the dough together firmly. Cover with a clean tea towel and leave to rise for approximately 1 hour. Brush with oil and place in the oven for 30 minutes or until nicely browned. Cut into slices and serve.

RED CABBAGE
Czerwona Kapusta

Serves 6

....

900 g (2 lb) red cabbage
1 tablespoon salt
25 g (1 oz) butter
25 g (1 oz) flour
150 ml (1/4 pint) red wine
2 teaspoons sugar
pinch of pepper
pinch of ground cloves
pinch of cinnamon

....

Chop the cabbage finely and sprinkle with salt. Leave for 15 minutes and rinse well. Put into a pan with boiling water (just enough to cover the cabbage but no more). Leave to simmer slowly until just tender. Drain, reserving a little of the liquid.

Make a roux with the butter and flour, adding a little of the cabbage liquid to thin it down to the consistency of double cream, and add it to the cabbage. Mix in all the other ingredients and simmer for a further 5 minutes before serving.

CAULIFLOWER À LA POLONAISE
Kalafior po Polsku

Serves 6

....

    1 large or 2 small cauliflowers
    salt
    50 g (2 oz) butter
    4 tablespoons dried breadcrumbs

....

    Wash the cauliflower and divide into florets. Cook in a little boiling salted water until just tender. Drain. Melt the butter and fry the breadcrumbs in it until golden; pour over the cauliflower just before serving.

POTATOES

Although not as popular as the cereals grown and eaten in Poland, potatoes are nevertheless an important part of the Polish diet. Potato soups, potato pancakes, potato cutlets and even potato doughnuts are much enjoyed. Potatoes came to Poland during the reign of Jan Sobieski when, following his victory over the Turks at the Battle of Vienna in 1683, he sent some potato tubers, which were being grown at the Emperor's residence in Vienna, to Poland to be planted at Wilanów, his summer residence. However, it was not until the reign of Augustus III (1734-63) that potatoes became widely known and liked. During this time many Germans settled on the Polish royal estates at the King's invitation, and they planted potatoes which became popular with the peasants. By the 1770s, vodka was being distilled from them, and they were an established ingredient in Polish cooking.

    In more modest Polish homes, potatoes in one form or another often make up the main part of the meal. This is rarely so in restaurants, where potaoes normally feature as an accompaniment. This is a shame because many potato recipes, particularly for potato pancakes, are among the nicest Polish dishes. It is necessary, therefore, to go to a private house and sample Polish hospitality in order to see the various ways in which potatoes are used. Sour cream and onions are their traditional partners, where variety exists in the finished product rather than in the basic ingredients. For example, the textures of the two versions of potato pancakes given on the following pages are quite different from each other even though the ingredients are almost the same. Potato cutlets are delicious and satisfying as a main dish, and so are potatoes baked in layers with eggs and mushrooms. They are also used simply as a vegetable on their own, and sliced into winter soups.

POTATO PANCAKES
Placki Kartoflane

Potato pancakes are a typical Polish dish, one of the best things you can eat in Poland, but restaurants seem to consider them too humble to appear on their menus. Princess Lew Sapieha showed me how to make two different types of pancake, both of which are given below. I prefer type I, the coarser and more unsophisticated of the two. Both should be eaten straight from the frying pan, ignoring all formalities like waiting for other people to have some to eat, so they are best eaten *en-famille* unless you have a very large frying pan, and can do them all at once.

POTATO PANCAKE I

Serves 4

2-3 large potatoes
1 small onion
salt and pepper
vegetable oil for frying
300 ml (¹/₂ pint) sour cream or 150 ml (¹/₄ pint)
sour cream and 150 ml (¹/₄ pint) yoghurt

Peel the potatoes and the onion and grate both coarsely. Mix well and squeeze out as much excess liquid as possible by putting the mixture in a sieve and pressing down with the back of a metal spoon. Season.

Pour enough oil into a large frying pan to cover the bottom generously. When really hot put in large spoonfuls of the potatoes and immediately flatten each one with the back of a spatula. They should be quite thin. When the underside is really dark brown, turn (but do not try to turn them too early, because they will disintegrate) and cook on the other side.

Serve with sour cream or, for a less rich accompaniment, sour cream mixed well with yoghurt.

POTATO PANCAKE II

This is more like an English pancake, both in taste and consistency.

Serves 4

2-3 large potatoes
1 egg
2-3 tablespoons plain flour
vegetable oil for frying
300 ml ($^1/_2$ pint) sour cream or 150 ml ($^1/_4$ pint)
  sour cream and 150 ml ($^1/_4$ pint) yoghurt

Grate the peeled potatoes finely, mix with the egg and stir in the flour until you have a loose consistency but one that holds its shape.

Heat the oil until very hot and pour large spoonfuls of the mixture into the pan, flattening out immediately to make sure each pancake is thin. Cook until well browned on both sides. Serve with sour cream or sour cream and yoghurt mixed.

POTATO CUTLETS
Kotlety Ziemniaczane

Serve these with a dill sauce (see page 115).

Serves 6

1.2 kg (2 lb 10$^1/_2$ oz) potatoes
2 eggs
50 g (2 oz) plain flour
50 g (2 oz) onion
25 g (1 oz) butter
salt and pepper
50 g (2 oz) dried breadcrumbs
butter or oil for frying

Peel and slice the potatoes, and boil until soft. Mash thoroughly and leave to cool. Mix in the eggs and flour. Dice the onion, fry in the butter until lightly browned and mix with the potatoes. Mash all again very thoroughly and season. Form the dough into a roll about 5 cm (2 in) thick and cut diagonally into 3-4 cm (1 in) pieces. Form into cutlets, coat them in breadcrumbs and fry on both sides in hot butter or oil until light brown.

Potatoes with Eggs and Mushrooms au Gratin
Kartofle Zapiekane z Jajami i Grzybami

Sliced tomatoes can be used instead of mushrooms.

Serves 4

....

1.2 kg (2 lb 10½ oz) potatoes
salt and pepper
250 g (9 oz) flat mushrooms
4-5 eggs
100 g (3½ oz) onion
50 g (2 oz) butter
butter for greasing
150 ml (¼ pint) single cream
150 g (5 oz) Cheddar cheese, grated
25 g (1 oz) breadcrumbs

....

Wash but do not peel or slice the potatoes. Drop into salted boiling water and cook until just tender. Drain and leave to cool, then peel and slice. Wash the mushrooms and slice them coarsely. Hard-boil the eggs, cool, peel and slice. Peel the onion and chop it roughly. Melt the butter and fry both the onions and mushrooms until soft.

Preheat the oven to 180C/350F/Gas 4. Grease an ovenproof dish and arrange in it layers of potatoes, mushrooms, eggs and onions, repeating until all have been used up. Finish with a layer of potatoes and season each layer well. Pour the cream on top and sprinkle with grated cheese and breadcrumbs. Bake for about 30 minutes, until heated right through and golden on top.

SAVOURY POTATO DOUGHNUTS
Pączki Ziemniaczane

This easy and very light potato dish is a good accompaniment to fish.

Serves 4

500 g (1¹/₄ lb) potatoes
salt and pepper
2 tablespoons sour cream
25 g (1 oz) butter
3 egg yolks
1 onion, peeled
4 tablespoons plain flour
butter for greasing
1 egg, beaten
breadcrumbs

Peel the potatoes and cook in plenty of salted boiling water. When soft, drain and mash well. To the potatoes add the sour cream, butter and egg yolks. Mix thoroughly. Pour boiling water over the onion and grate it finely into the potatoes. Mix in the flour and season.

Preheat the oven to 180C/350F/Gas 4. Grease a baking tray and put tablespoons of the potato mixture on it. Brush with beaten egg. Sprinkle breadcrumbs lightly on top of each 'doughnut' and place in the oven for 20 minutes until nicely browned.

CUCUMBER

CUCUMBER STUFFED WITH HONEY
Ogórek Nadziewany Miodem

This is apparently a Lithuanian dish. Served at teatime, it makes a very refreshing summer snack.

Serves 4

> **1 cucumber**
> **set honey to fill**
> **sour cream or cream to serve**

Remove the skin from the cucumber, halve it lengthways and deseed. Fill the hollow in the centre with honey, cut the cucumber into portions and chill in the refrigerator until needed. Serve with sour cream or cream.

PICKLED CUCUMBERS
Ogórki Kiszone

This is Stefan Komornicki's recipe for souring cucumbers. without using vinegar. It was given to me by Stefan's father, Juliusz Komornicki. Juliusz's great grandfather originating from Germany founded the large brewery, Okocim, and purchased the estate there shortly afterwards. This estate belonging to Juliusz's mother's family was the scene of many a good day's shooting. They took their patriotism sufficiently seriously to add the name Okocimski to their original name Goetz, and the brewery still operates to this day. Indeed, Okocim beer can easily be purchased in England.

The best cucumbers for this recipe are the small, very bumpy ones, but long cucumbers will do, cut to size.

Serves 6

....

6 small cucumbers (ideally 7.5-10 cm (3-4 in) long)
2 x ¹/₂ litre (scant 1 pint) jars with lids

For each jar:
2 cloves garlic
10 cm (4 in) dill plant with some of the flower
1 small piece of horseradish root or 1 horseradish
  leaf or 1 cherry leaf

For the brine:
1 litre (1³/₄ pints) water
25 g (1 oz) salt

....

Wash the cucumbers in cold water with a brush. Wash the jars out with boiling water and leave upside down to drain.

Peel the garlic and put with the cucumbers and the other ingredients into the jars, packing tightly if necessary.

Prepare the brine. Bring the water and salt to the boil, remove from the heat and allow to cool a little. Pour into the jars, right up to the brim, and seal tightly with the lids at once.

Keep the jars in a dark place at room temperature for 2-3 weeks, checking each week that the tops are still on tightly. (They will last up to a year if kept in a cool, dark store cupboard.) Serve with cold meats and salads.

SALADS

Salads are gradually becoming more popular in Poland, and, although they are not eaten as widely as vegetables or cereals, they are enjoyed throughout the year. The favourite is probably cucumber salad (*mizeria*) which normally accompanies such classic dishes as Polish roast chicken. The more wintry beetroot and horseradish salad (*ćwikła*) is an ancient dish and is also often served, and goes particularly well with cold meats or sausage.

For these salads, Poles have created their own garnishes – diced hard-boiled egg and chopped fresh dill being the most common – and dressings, of which the most frequently used are sour cream or the delicious and rather unusual oil, lemon and egg dressing.

CUCUMBER SALAD
Mizeria

This popular salad has many legends attached to its name, all of them based on Queen Bona Sforza's love and vast consumption of it. It was called *mizeria* (misery in Latin), according to some, because Bona Sforza cried from homesickness for her native Italy while eating it. Others say she ate so much of it that she suffered from indigestion and would ask for a misericord – a dagger for committing suicide – to relieve her of her pain.

Serves 4

1 large cucumber
150 ml (¹/₄ pint) sour cream (single cream can
    be used, in which case increase the amount of
    lemon juice)
1 teaspoon salt
juice of ¹/₂ lemon

To garnish:
2 tablespoons freshly chopped dill

Peel and thinly slice the cucumber. Put in a colander, sprinkle with salt and leave for 30 minutes for the juices to drain. Rinse and pat dry.

Arrange the cucumber in a salad dish. Make a dressing from the sour cream and lemon juice, pour over the cucumber and sprinkle with dill.

TOMATOES STUFFED WITH CUCUMBER SALAD
Pomidory Nadziewane Ogórkiem

Serves 6

1 medium-sized cucumber
salt and pepper
300 ml (¹/₂ pint) sour cream
6 large beef tomatoes
1 tablespoon dill, chopped

Peel and slice the cucumber thickly. Put in a colander, sprinkle with salt and leave to drain for 30 minutes. Press out the juices, pat dry and dice. Add the sour cream, pepper and salt, and mix well. Wash the tomatoes and slice off the tops. With a spoon, scoop out the inside of the tomatoes and discard. Fill the hollows with the cucumber mixture and sprinkle dill over. Replace the tomato tops and serve.

LETTUCE SALAD
Sałata po Polsku

Serves 6

2 crisp lettuces

For the dressing:
150 ml (¹/₄ pint) sour cream
1 tablespoon chopped dill
a little lemon juice
salt and sugar to taste

To garnish:
2 eggs, hard-boiled and diced

Separate the leaves of the lettuce and wash and dry it thoroughly. Arrange in a salad bowl. Mix the ingredients for the dressing, pour over the salad and toss well. Sprinkle the diced eggs over and serve.

COTTAGE CHEESE SALAD
Majufes

I had this at a lovely old farmhouse in the Polish countryside. Jewish in origin, it makes an excellent summer lunch dish and is a refreshing alternative to an ordinary green salad.

Serves 4 as a starter or side dish

> 454 g (1 lb) cottage cheese
> 1/2 large cucumber
> 3 small tomatoes
> 1 green pepper
> 1 red pepper
> 150 ml (1/4 pint) sour cream
> 50 g (2 oz) Cheddar cheese

Put the cottage cheese into a salad bowl. Dice the vegetables and mix in. Stir in the sour cream and grate the cheese on top. Cover and leave in the refrigerator until needed.

CAULIFLOWER SALAD
Sałatka z Kalafiórw

Serves 4

> 1 large cauliflower
> salt and sugar to taste
> dash of vinegar
> 250 ml (scant 1/2 pint) mayonnaise (see page 121)
> 1 tablespoon chopped parsley

Wash the cauliflower and cook it in a little boiling water with a pinch of salt and sugar and a dash of vinegar. When just tender, drain and divide into small florets. Leave to cool. Put the cauliflower in a salad dish, pour over the mayonnaise and sprinkle with parsley.

RED CABBAGE SALAD
Sałatka z Czerwonej Kapusty

A cheerful and crunchy winter salad.

Serves 8

> **1 large red cabbage**
> **2 apples**
> **2 onions**
> **juice of 2 lemons**
> **1 teaspoon sugar**
> **1 teaspoon salt**

Cut the red cabbage into thin slices. Put into a little cold water and bring to the boil. Simmer for 10 minutes. Dice the apples and peel and dice the onions. Drain the cabbage and pour on the lemon juice. Toss well. As soon as the cabbage changes colour from bright red to dull red, add the apples and onions. Mix well and add the sugar and salt. Toss again and leave to cool.

BEETROOT AND HORSERADISH SALAD
Ćwikła

This is a classic Polish salad with ancient origins: a recipe for it – very similar to the one below – has been found dating from over 400 years ago.

Serves 6

> **6 young cooked beetroot**
> **3 tablespoons freshly grated horseradish**
> **salt**
> **2 tablespoons wine vinegar**

Peel and finely grate the beetroot. In a salad bowl arrange alternate layers of beetroot and very thinly scattered horseradish. Sprinkle with salt and pour over a little wine vinegar diluted with a splash of water. Leave in a cool place for 24 hours before serving.

Beetroot Salad
Sałatka z Buraków

This unusual dish combines two different salad dressings and perfectly balances sweet and sour.

Serves 6

....

600 g (1 lb 5 oz) cooked beetroot
15 cocktail gherkins
salt and pepper

For the vinaigrette:
3 tablespoons olive oil
1 tablespoon vinegar
1 teaspoon French mustard
pinch of sugar
salt and pepper

For the salad dressing:
150 ml (1/4 pint) sour cream
handful chopped fresh dill
1 teaspoon sugar

....

Slice the beetroot and gherkins, put into a china salad bowl (beetroot can stain wood) and season. Mix the vinaigrette and toss the beetroot thoroughly in it. Leave in the refrigerator for 20 minutes.

Mix the salad dressing and pour over the beetroot. Toss thoroughly and serve at once.

SAUCES

Most Polish sauces are derived from the herbs and seasonings that grow in the countryside. Chives, dill, mushrooms, juniper berries, rosehips and horseradish all have sauces of their own and play an important role in Polish cooking.

Juniper or rosehip sauce is the traditional accompaniment to game, while others are used frequently with meats, hot or cold, and dill sauce is also popular with fish. Tartare sauce and mayonnaise are not unique to the Polish kitchen, but are eaten widely with fish and salads. Polish Cumberland sauce is wonderfully rich and full-bodied, with its addition of orange rind. The smell of frying orange rind is exquisite in itself, and the taste is superb. As oranges are very expensive and hard to find in Poland, the orange eater tends to keep the skin for further use. This might mean candying it, sprinkling it over warm doughnuts or making a savoury sauce such as Cumberland sauce, to go with cold meats. Caramel is used quite often in sauces, mostly as a colouring agent, but also for its flavour.

Garnishes such as dried breadcrumbs or diced hard-boiled eggs will often be mixed into or sprinkled over the top of a sauce as a finishing touch.

Mushroom Sauce
Sos Grzybowy

This can also be made with dried mushrooms, using 40 g (1¹/₂ oz) of dried mushrooms, rinsed well and soaked in lukewarm water for 30 minutes. Drain, dice and proceed as below.

Serves 4, making approximately 175 ml (6 fl oz)

1 onion, peeled and diced
25 g (1 oz) butter
250 g (8 oz) flat mushrooms, washed and chopped
1 tablespoon lemon juice
salt and pepper
1 tablespoon plain flour
50 ml (2 fl oz) milk
150 ml (¹/₄ pint) sour cream

Cook the onion in the butter until soft. Add the mushrooms and stir in the lemon juice. Turn down the heat, cover the pan and simmer very slowly for 10 minutes. Season. Mix the flour with the milk to achieve a smooth paste, and stir into the mushrooms. Simmer for a further 5 minutes, stirring frequently. Mix in the sour cream and heat through without boiling. Serve.

CHIVE SAUCE
Sos Szczypiórkowy

This is excellent with lamb cutlets or boiled beef.

Makes approximately 300 ml (¹/₂ pint)

25 g (1 oz) butter
1 tablespoon flour
300 ml (¹/₂ pint) beef stock
1 tablespoon wine vinegar
1 tablespoon caramel (see page 123)
2 tablespoons chopped chives
salt and sugar to taste

Melt the butter, add the flour and allow to brown a little. Stir in the beef stock gradually until you have a smooth, thickish sauce. Add the vinegar and the caramel. Stir the chives into the stock, and sprinkle in a little salt and sugar to taste. Bring to the boil and simmer for about 3 minutes before serving.

DILL SAUCE
Sos Koperkowy

This sauce is often served with Boiled Brisket of Beef (see page 63) and goes well with most fish dishes.

Makes approximately 300 ml (¹/₂ pint)

25 g (1 oz) butter
1 tablespoon flour
300 ml (¹/₂ pint) chicken stock or milk
2 teaspoons lemon juice
2 heaped tablespoons chopped fresh dill

Make a roux with the butter and flour and gradually add the stock or milk until it is the consistency of single cream. Stir in the lemon juice and bring to the boil, and when bubbling add the dill. Simmer for about 3 minutes before serving.

JUNIPER SAUCE
Sos z Jałowca

The juniper berry, popular and much used in the Polish kitchen —
particularly with game — is immortalised in a romantic song from eastern
Poland in which a wounded Cossack lies underneath a juniper tree,
thinking about his girlfriend far away.

Serves 8

1/2 **carrot**
1 **medium-sized onion, peeled**
2 **rashers bacon**
50 g (2 oz) **butter**
2 1/2 **tablespoons juniper berries**
500 ml (scant 1 pint) **game stock**
300 ml (1/2 pint) **dry white wine**
1 **tablespoon double cream (optional)**
salt and pepper

Chop the carrot into thick slices. Dice the onion and chop the
bacon. Melt the butter in a pan and add the vegetables, bacon and juniper
berries. Stir well. Cook until the onions and bacon are lightly browned.
Pour in the stock and leave, uncovered, on a low heat to cook for one hour,
stirring from time to time. Strain the sauce, mix in the white wine (and the
double cream if wanted). Season to taste. Pour into a sauceboat and serve.

ROSEHIP SAUCE
Sos z Dzikiej Róży

This is a favourite sauce with game.

Makes approximately 750 ml (1¹/₄ pints)

300 ml (¹/₂ pint) rosehips (gathered after the first frost)
25 g (1 oz) butter
1 heaped tablespoon plain flour
300 ml (¹/₂ pint) game stock
150 ml (¹/₄ pint) red wine
4 juniper berries
1 bayleaf
2 cloves
sugar to taste
salt and pepper

Wash the rosehips, and remove the stalks and calyces. Put in a pan and just cover with cold water and bring to the boil. Simmer until tender. Liquidise. Melt the butter, stir in the flour and allow to cook over a low heat for a few minutes. Gradually add the stock, the wine, the puréed rosehips and the seasonings. Cook gently for 30 minutes. Strain and serve.

VENISON SAUCE
Sos z Sarny

This is an excellent way of using up venison leftovers, and is good with pork dishes.

Serves 6

450 g (1 lb) leftover roasted venison
1 heaped tablespoon plain flour
750 ml (1¼ pints) venison stock made from the bones
150 ml (¼ pint) red wine
a little chopped lemon peel
250 ml (scant ½ pint) cream
salt and pepper

Mince the meat and mix with the flour. Place in a pan and slowly stir in the stock. Bring to the boil, add the wine, lemon peel, cream and seasonings and simmer for about 3 minutes before serving.

WILD PLUM SAUCE
Sos z Dzikich Śliwek

Wild plums taste completely different from ordinary plums – much stronger and earthier. Wild plum jam or extract is quite easy to buy in country shops, and in large food departments in London. This sauce is an ideal accompaniment to wild boar or pork.

Makes approximately 150 ml (1 pint)

200 ml (7 fl oz) beef stock
3 tablespoons wild plum jam
3 cloves, crushed
pinch cinnamon
sugar to taste
dash of red wine
salt and pepper

Heat the beef stock in a saucepan. Stir in the other ingredients and bring to the boil. Allow to simmer until the sauce has reduced slightly, and serve.

POLISH CUMBERLAND SAUCE
Cumberland Sauce à la Polonaise

Polish Cumberland sauce differs from the English variety in many ways. It does not include mustard, port or arrowroot but fried orange rind, which increases the rich spiciness that goes so well with cold meats.

Makes approximately 300 ml (¹/₂ pint)

> **1-2 tablespoons horseradish cream or sauce**
> **4 tablespoons redcurrant jelly or bilberry jam**
> **1 tablespoon lemon juice**
> **pinch of salt**
> **25 g (1 oz) butter**
> **rind of 1 orange**

Mix together the horseradish cream, redcurrant jelly, lemon juice and salt. Melt the butter in a small frying pan. Remove as much pith from the orange rind as possible, chop the rind finely and fry lightly in the butter. Mix into the sauce.

Serve with cold meats, pâtés, etc.

MUSTARD SAUCE
Sos Musztardowy

Serve with cold meats or Roast Eel (see page 48).

Makes approximately 100 ml (scant ¹/₄ pint)

> **4 hard-boiled egg yolks**
> **1 tablespoon Dijon mustard**
> **100 ml (scant ¹/₄ pint) good olive oil**
> **pinch of salt**
> **pinch of sugar**

Crush the yolks and mix with the mustard until smooth. Pour the oil on to the yolks in a slow and steady stream, whisking constantly. Add the salt and sugar.

HOT HORSERADISH SAUCE
Sos Chrzanowy

This is the traditional accompaniment to Boiled Brisket of Beef (see page 63).

Makes approximately 300 ml (¹/₂ pint)

....

> 25 g (1 oz) butter
> ³/₄ tablespoon flour
> 150 ml (¹/₄ pint) beef stock
> 1 tablespoon lemon juice
> ¹/₂ teaspoon sugar
> 2 teaspoons freshly grated horseradish

....

Melt the butter, add the flour and cook over a gentle heat for a few minutes. Gradually stir in the beef stock, then add the lemon juice and sugar. Mix in the horseradish. Reheat if necessary, without allowing the sauce to boil, and serve.

COLD HORSERADISH SAUCE
Sos Chrzanowy

Serve with beef or wild boar.

Makes approximately 300 ml (¹/₂ pint)

....

> 1 hard-boiled egg yolk
> pinch of salt
> pinch of sugar
> 1 tablespoon lemon juice
> 150 ml (¹/₄ pint) sour cream
> 2 teaspoons freshly grated horseradish

....

Mash the egg yolk and mix with the other ingredients.

Opposite: Cabbage Parcels (*Gołabki*)

GREEN HORSERADISH SAUCE
Zielony Sos Chrzanowy

Makes approximately 300 ml (¹/₂ pint)

2 tablespoons freshly grated horseradish
150 ml (¹/₄ pint) double cream
pinch of salt
¹/₂ teaspoon sugar
2 eggs, hard-boiled
2 tablespoons fresh chives, chopped
2 tablespoons fresh dill, chopped
2 tablespoons watercress, chopped

Mix the horseradish with the cream, salt and sugar. Shell the eggs, mash the yolks thoroughly and add them to the horseradish mixture. Dice the egg whites and mix with the chopped chives, dill and watercress. Fold into the sauce and serve.

MAYONNAISE
Majonez

Makes approximately 300 ml (¹/₂ pint)

4 hard-boiled egg yolks
4 raw egg yolks
150 ml (¹/₄ pint) olive oil
lemon juice to taste
salt and pepper

Mash the hard-boiled yolks thoroughly and mix with the raw yolks. Pour in the oil in a steady trickle, whisking all the time, until the sauce is white and smooth. Add lemon juice, salt and pepper. Place in the refrigerator until needed. This mayonnaise will keep for up to 10 days.

Opposite: Hunter's Stew (*Bigos*)

TARTARE SAUCE
Sos Tatarski

Makes approximately 250 ml (scant ¹/₂ pint)

> 200 g (7 oz) mayonnaise (see page 121)
> 5 teaspoons French mustard
> 1 tablespoon capers
> 2 small pickled cucumbers, finely chopped
> 1 tablespoon lemon juice
> salt and pepper

Mix all the above ingredients together and serve chilled.

BUTTER SAUCE FOR FISH
Sos Jajeczny

This exquisite sauce is frequently used at Christmas and goes well with pike and carp. It is not one for the faint-hearted!

Serves 8

> 6 eggs
> 250 g (9 oz) butter
> salt and pepper

Boil the eggs for 10 minutes. Shell and chop them. Melt the butter. Put the eggs in a sauceboat and pour the butter over them. Season and serve at once.

EGG DRESSING FOR SALADS
Przyprowa do Sałatek z Jajkiem

Used as an alternative to sour cream dressing, this is another typical Polish dressing.

Serves 4

1 egg, hard-boiled
3 tablespoons olive oil
juice of 1/2 lemon
1/2 teaspoon sugar

Shell the egg, cut it in half and remove the yolk. Mash the yolk to a smooth paste with the oil and add the lemon juice and sugar. Chop the egg whites and mix them in. Pour over the salad and toss well.

CARAMEL
Karmel

Caramel is often used in Polish cookery to colour sauces for meat dishes.

150 g (5 oz) granulated sugar
75 ml (2¹/₂ fl oz) water

Pour the sugar and water into a heavy pan and stir over a medium flame. Continue to stir while the sugar dissolves and starts to turn golden. After a few minutes it will bubble and froth, but continue to stir and leave to cook until it turns a rich honey colour. If a sweet taste is required the caramel should be removed from the heat at this point and used. If it is simply needed to colour a sauce, however, without sweetening it, let it cook a little longer until deep brown in colour. Remove from the heat and use as required.

BÉCHAMEL SAUCE
Sos Beszamelowy

Makes approximately 300 ml (¹/₂ pint)

300 ml (¹/₂ pint) milk
¹/₂ small bay leaf
sprig of thyme
¹/₂ small onion
¹/₄ level teaspoon grated nutmeg
25 g (1 oz) butter
25 g (1 oz) plain flour
2 tablespoons single cream
salt and black pepper

Pour the milk into a heavy-based saucepan, add the bay leaf, thyme, onion and nutmeg and slowly bring to the boil. Remove from the heat, cover tightly and leave for 15 minutes for the flavours to infuse.

In a separate pan, melt the butter. With a wooden spoon, stir in the flour and cook over a gentle heat for 3 minutes.

Strain the milk through a fine sieve and add it, little by little, to the flour-and-butter roux, stirring all the time. Bring to the boil, stirring continuously, and simmer for 2-3 minutes. Stir in the cream and season to taste.

PANCAKES
AND PUDDINGS

A wide variety of puddings is eaten in Poland, and they form a vital part of the Polish meal. Pancakes are perhaps the most typical of them all. Uniquely light when made with beaten egg white, they are eaten with a sweet and sour filling such as jam or curd cheese, and make a classic finish to any meal.

Fruit is used in most puddings, and is also often eaten on its own, poached in a light syrup with a sweet sauce. Fresh fruit of good quality is hard to buy in the shops, so tinned fruit is more often used although it is expensive as it is chiefly found in hard-currency shops. In summer, fruit jellies are popular. Made from any available fruit, they are refreshing and easy to eat. Also in the category of puddings that slip down easily are the various coffee or cocoa baked milks, and the deliciously moist semolina pudding.

Puddings in Poland are very tasty, healthy, and relatively simple, culinary complexities are left for making pastries.

POLISH PANCAKES
Naleśniki

These pancakes are beautifully light and fluffy due to the addition of beaten egg whites. They can, alternatively, be served with jam.

Serves 6

For the pancakes:
225 g (8 oz) plain flour
1 egg
3 eggs, separated
300 ml (¹/₂ pint) milk
300 ml (¹/₂ pint) water
1 tablespoon oil
pinch of nutmeg
1 level teaspoon salt
25 g (1 oz) lard for greasing

For the filling:
250 g (9 oz) curd cheese
25 g (1 oz) butter
1 egg yolk
sugar to taste (approximately 1 level teaspoon)
pinch of vanilla sugar
milk

To make the batter, sift the flour into a large bowl, add the egg and the egg yolks. Stir in the milk, water, oil and nutmeg. Mix together thoroughly. Whisk the egg whites with the salt until stiff, and fold into the batter.

Smear the bottom of a pancake or heavy-based frying pan with lard, enough to make the bottom of the pan sparkle. When piping hot, pour in a ladleful of batter and cook on both sides until lightly browned. Continue until all the batter has been used up, keeping the pancakes warm in a low oven.

To make the filling, push the curd cheese through a sieve, cream the butter with the egg yolk and add to the cheese. Add sugar and vanilla sugar. Stir in a little milk if the mixture is too stiff.

Put a spoonful of the filling on each pancake, fold over and serve hot.

BOILED PANCAKES
Naleśniki Gotowane

These pancakes, cooked in milk, make a pleasant change from the fried variety. Their light, moist, bland texture is reminiscent of nursery food, and they are, as a result very easily digested. A tart fresh fruit or jam accompaniment makes an excellent contrast.

Serves 2

25 g (1 oz) plain flour
2 eggs
2 teaspoons caster sugar
750 ml (1¹/₄ pints) milk

To garnish:
fresh strawberries or raspberries or any fruit jam
whipped cream

Sift the flour and mix with the eggs and sugar until smooth. In a pan wide enough to cook all the pancakes at once, bring the milk to the boil and spoon tablespoonfuls of the batter on to the milk. The mixture should make about 6. Simmer for several minutes until set.

These can be eaten either with fresh fruit, such as strawberries or raspberries – put on to one pancake and topped by another – or with a little jam. Both versions should be served with a little whipped cream.

SAXON PANCAKES
Naleśniki po Sasku

This recipe from Wierzyriek's restaurant in Cracow is named after the short dynasty of Saxon Kings which ruled in the eighteenth century. Judging by a saying of those days, 'Under the Saxon King, eat, drink and loosen your belt', this rich dish of pancakes filled with curd cheese, served with whipped cream, fruits of the season, grated chocolate and sultanas, is clearly appropriately titled. With the addition of a little sugar soaked in alcohol to the finished dish, it can even be served aflame.

Serves 10

For the pancakes:
300 g (10^1/$_2$ oz) plain flour
3 eggs
300 ml (^{1}/$_2$ pint) milk
300 ml (^{1}/$_2$ pint) water
pinch of salt
25 g (1 oz) słonina (pork fat) or lard for greasing

For the filling:
700 g (1 lb 8 oz) curd cheese
3 eggs
200 g (7 oz) icing sugar
10 g (^{1}/$_4$-^{1}/$_2$ oz) vanilla sugar
50 g (2 oz) sultanas

100 g (3^1/$_2$ oz) butter
50 g (2 oz) icing sugar
25 g (1 oz) cranberry sauce or 500 g (1 lb 2 oz)
   canned or fresh peaches or 500 g (1 lb 2 oz)
   canned or fresh pineapple
300 g (10^1/$_2$ oz) whipped cream
50 g (2 oz) grated chocolate
50 g (2 oz) sultanas

To make the batter, sift the flour, add the eggs and milk and mix until smooth. Stir in the water and salt. To make the pancakes, rub a pancake or heavy-based frying pan with *słonina* or lard until the surface sparkles. When piping hot, pour a ladleful of batter in at a time and fry on both sides until lightly browned. Continue until all the batter is used up.

To make the filling push the curd cheese through a sieve, mix with the eggs and stir in the other ingredients. Spread inside the pancakes and fold them over twice to make triangular shapes.

To serve, melt the butter in a pan and warm the pancakes quickly in this. Arrange on a plate and serve sprinkled with icing sugar, decorated with cranberry sauce, peaches or pineapples, and whipped cream. Top with grated chocolate and sultanas.

PANCAKES WITH MULLED WINE
Naleśniki Litewskie

This recipe uses the same batter as the one on page 126, but here the pancakes are cut into strips, flavoured with sugar and cinnamon and served with a sweet red wine sauce.

Serves 6

....

1 quantity pancake batter (see page 126)
2-3 tablespoons caster sugar
pinch of cinnamon

For the sauce:
6 egg yolks
4 tablespoons caster sugar
300 ml (¹/₂ pint) red wine

....

Make the pancakes as described on page 126. Cut the cooked pancakes into strips and place them in a pot, layering them with sugar and cinnamon. Put in a low oven to keep hot.

To make the sauce, whisk the egg yolks with the sugar until pale and fluffy. Over a low heat, add the wine and continue to whisk. When the sauce bubbles and froths, pour over the pancakes and serve.

Pears in Vanilla Sauce
Gruszki w Sosie Waniliowym

Vanilla was probably introduced to Poland in the early Renaissance period by the Armenian traders who brought spices from the East.

Tinned pears are not essential to this recipe, but as tinned fruit is more available in Poland than fresh fruit it is used widely. If you have fresh pears, follow the cooking instructions on page 131, reserving 300 ml (1/2 pint) of the cooking liquid, and continue as follows.

Serves 8

....

> 840 g (1 lb 14 oz) tinned pears in syrup
> 2 eggs
> 100 g (3^{1}/$_{2}$ oz) caster sugar
> 25 g (1 oz) cornflour
> 150 ml (1/4 pint) milk
> 1/2 vanilla pod

....

Drain the pears, reserving 300 ml (1/2 pint) of the syrup. Whisk the eggs with the sugar and cornflour in a glass bowl. Put the milk in a pan, add the vanilla and bring to the boil. Pour the syrup from the pears into a separate pan and also bring to the boil. Remove the milk from the heat and pour slowly over the beaten eggs. Follow with the syrup. Mix all this together thoroughly, stand the bowl over boiling water and stir until it has thickened to a cream. Cool and pour over the pears.

PEARS IN RED WINE SAUCE
Gruszki w Sosie Winnym

This is one of the most delicious sauces and goes beautifully with pears. It is sweet without being sickly and light rather than cloying. Simple to do, it gives the impression of hidden complexities.

Serves 4

---

4 just ripe dessert pears
175 g (6 oz) caster sugar
6 egg yolks
1¹/₂ glasses red wine

Peel and quarter the pears. Bring a little water to the boil, add half the caster sugar and cook the pears in this until tender. Strain, discarding the syrup. Arrange the pears on warm pudding plates. In a saucepan, beat the egg yolks with the remaining sugar until they are pale. Mix in the wine and heat gently, whisking all the time. When the foam rises, pour the sauce over the pears and serve.

STUFFED PLUMS
Śliwki Nadziewane

Serves 4

....

> 12 ripe plums
> 110 g (4 oz) curd cheese
> 1 egg yolk
> 3 teaspoons caster sugar
> cream to serve (optional)

....

Heat the oven to 180C/350F/Gas 4. Halve and stone the plums. Force the curd cheese through a sieve to break it up slightly. Beat the egg yolk with the sugar until white and fluffy, and mix with the curd cheese. Spoon this mixture into the hollows of the plums, and put in the oven for 40 minutes. Serve hot, with cream, if wanted.

APRICOT DELIGHT
Rozkosz z Moreli

This decorative cake is rich, filling and wonderfully crunchy.

Serves 6-8

....

> 225 g (8 oz) dried apricots
> 225 g (8 oz) caster sugar
> 110 g (4 oz) almonds, chopped
> 50 g (2 oz) candied orange peel
> icing sugar for coating

....

Pour cold water over the apricots until they are just covered and leave to soak overnight. The next day pour the apricots and water into a saucepan, add the sugar and bring to the boil. Simmer for about 45 minutes until the mixture is thick. Stir in the almonds and orange peel. Sprinkle some icing sugar on to a board, form the apricot mixture into a long roll about 5 cm (2 in) thick, and coat in icing sugar. Leave to dry for several hours in a cool place. Slice and serve.

APPLE FRITTERS
Jabłka Smażone w Cieście

These apple crescents, dipped in batter, melt in the mouth.

Serves 2-4

For the batter:
2 eggs, separated
40 g (1½ oz) caster sugar
5 tablespoons single cream
110 g (4 oz) plain flour
1 tablespoon cornflour

450 g (1 lb) cooking apples
110 g (4 oz) butter or oil
icing sugar

To make the batter, beat the egg yolks with sugar and cream. Whisk the egg whites until very stiff and fold in. Sift the flours and mix in lightly.

Peel, core and cut the apples into rings. Spike the apple rings and turn in the batter. Melt the butter or heat the oil in a frying pan, and drop the apple rings into it. Fry on both sides until golden and nicely puffed up. Pile on a plate, sprinkle icing sugar over them through a fine sieve and serve at once.

MERINGUES
Bezy

This is a wonderful way of using up egg whites, and any amount can be used provided you follow the proportions given here. The Poles fill them with whipped cream and fruit and serve them as a pudding.

Makes 20

1 mug of egg whites
butter for greasing the baking tray
2 mugs of caster sugar
flour to sprinkle on the baking tray

Preheat the oven to 180C/350F/Gas 4. Whip the egg whites until fairly stiff. Mix half the sugar into the egg whites and whip again until very stiff. Fold in the rest of the sugar. Grease a baking tray and sprinkle it lightly with flour, shaking off any excess. Spoon the mixture into a forcing bag and pipe small mounds on to the baking tray. Put the tray in the oven and immediately turn it down to its lowest setting. Cook for 1 hour, when the meringues should be lightly browned and firm to the touch.

FRUIT JELLY
Kisiel

This Russian pudding is popular in Poland and simple to make. It can be made with any fruit, but those with a tart flavour are best. Potato flour is a thickening agent and gives the pudding the consistency of jelly. This is a deliciously moist concoction and makes a refreshing end to a meal. It can be served, turned out of the ramekin dishes, with a little sweetened milk – whisked with an egg yolk to thicken it – or a vanilla sauce.

Serves 6

500 g (1 lb 2 oz) cranberries or redcurrants
50 g (2 oz) potato flour
150 ml ($1/4$ pint) water
sugar to taste

Wash and hull the fruit. Cook in boiling water until soft, then push through a sieve or liquidise. Mix the potato flour with 150 ml ($1/4$ pint) water and stir into the hot fruit. Bring to the boil, stirring constantly, and add sugar to taste. Spoon into ramekin dishes and chill.

PASKHA I
Pascha

Paskha is the Russian word for Easter, and it is also what they call this rich dessert which is traditionally served on that day. *Paskha* is sometimes eaten in Poland at Easter, and I have seen and eaten various alternatives to the original (see page 177) with, for example, a finishing layer of jelly or a biscuit base, but, with the exception of the one included here, never found them as nice. The consistency of the authentic version should be that of a dense mousse, so that the pudding holds together when unmoulded, but this variation is more liquid in consistency. It is quicker to make as none of the ingredients is heated at any point, and is lighter than the standard version, although similar in taste. Sheer heaven to eat, this pudding needs no accompaniment, but should not be eaten at the end of a rich meal.

Paskha needs to be prepared the day before it is to be eaten.

Serves 8-10

1 kg (2¼ lb) curd cheese
250 g (9 oz) butter
½ vanilla pod
7 egg yolks
350 g (12¼ oz) caster sugar
2 tablespoons mixed nuts, chopped
2 tablespoons almonds, chopped
2 tablespoons dried figs, chopped
2 tablespoons raisins
2 tablespoons orange rind, chopped

Cream the curd cheese with the butter, mixing thoroughly. Grate the vanilla to a powder and mix in. Beat the yolks with the sugar until white and add to cheese mixture. Stir in the remaining ingredients. Pour into a suitable container and leave in the refrigerator for 24 hours. Serve from the bowl.

COFFEE CREAM
Budyń Kawowy

Serves 8

20 g (³/₄ oz) freshly ground coffee
750 ml (1¹/₄ pints) milk
¹/₂ level tablespoon sugar
4 eggs

Preheat the oven to 200C/400F/Gas 6. Pour 150 ml (1 pint) of boiling water over the ground coffee, stir and leave to settle. When the coffee sinks to the bottom, filter it. Mix the coffee with the milk and add sugar. Break the eggs into the milk and mix thoroughly. Pour into 8 ramekin dishes and place them on a baking tray half-filled with boiling water. Put into the oven for 45 minutes until set and lightly browned on top. Remove and cool before serving.

WHIPPED CREAM CHARLOTTE
Krem Cytrynowy

This is a deliciously alcoholic pudding, creamy in texture. Sandwich between crisp biscuity wafers (*Tortenbödon*), which can be bought from any Polish delicatessen.

Serves 8

2 round cake wafers approximately 24 cm
  (9¹/₂ in) in diameter
500 ml (scant 1 pint) double cream
125 g (4¹/₂ oz) caster sugar
500 ml (scant 1 pint) maraschino liqueur
25 g (1 oz) lemon jelly
150 ml (¹/₄ pint) water
fresh fruit to decorate

Line the bottom of a cake tin or flan dish with one of the wafers. Whisk the cream and the sugar until stiff, and stir in the maraschino. Dissolve the jelly in lukewarm water and mix in as well. Pour into the flan dish and top with the remaining wafer. Chill for several hours. Decorate with fresh fruit of the season before serving.

APPLE COMPOTE
Kompot z Jabłek

Compotes are cold fruit desserts, sweet in flavour because the fruit is cooked in syrup. Much loved in Poland and very healthy, they can be made from any fruit, but tart fruits which hold their shape during cooking are best. Raspberries, for example, are not ideal as they easily cook to a pulp full of seeds, and also lose their colour. The best fruits are apples, pears, sweet or sour cherries, greengages, plums, blueberries, currants and gooseberries. Two or more fruits can be mixed and, indeed, often are.

Apple Compote is sometimes also served in small quantities with roast chicken.

Serves 4

150 g (5 oz) caster sugar
500 ml (scant 1 pint) water
1/2 teaspoon cinnamon
6 cloves
500 g (1 lb 2 oz) cooking apples

Make a syrup from the sugar and water by putting them in a pan over a low heat and stirring constantly until the sugar has dissolved. Add the cinnamon and cloves. Wash and peel the apples, divide into quarters and remove the cores. Bring the syrup to the boil, add the apples – just enough to cover the surface in one-layer – and simmer gently until soft. Cook the apples in batches if necessary. Place the apples in a compote dish, pour the syrup over them and serve cool.

Semolina Pudding
Budyń Grysikowy

This is a lighter, moister and fluffier version of English semolina pudding.

Serves 4

125 g (4¹/₂ oz) caster sugar
3 eggs
grated rind of ¹/₂ lemon
125 g (4¹/₂ oz) semolina
butter for greasing
300 ml (¹/₂ pint) milk

Preheat the oven to 180C/350F/Gas 4. Beat the sugar with the eggs until they are pale and fluffy. Mix in the lemon rind and semolina. Lightly butter a soufflé dish and pour in the mixture. Bake for 20-30 minutes, until set. Remove from the oven. Bring the milk to a boil and pour over the semolina pudding. Do not stir. The milk will be absorbed, giving the pudding a light, creamy texture. Serve at once.

CAKES AND PASTRIES

As a nation, Poles have a sweet tooth. Cakes and pastries are nibbled throughout the day in cafés and at home, with morning coffee or afternoon tea. They are also frequently served as a pudding course at the end of a meal. Special occasions such as Christmas, Easter, Shrove Tuesday or Epiphany are all marked with particular confections. Poppy Seed Roll (*makowiec,* page 196) is always eaten at Christmas; *babkis* and *mazurki* (pages 175 and 172) are traditionally associated with Easter. Doughnuts (*pączki,* page 140), like our pancakes, are the typical fare for Shrove Tuesday, and also for Epiphany and New Year's Eve.

Of all the sweet recipes, the one with the most variations on a theme is the popular national cake *mazurek*. Not only are there different methods for the preparation of the pastry, there is also an endless range of toppings. I have seen fourteen in one handwritten family cookbook, and this is not unusual.

Nuts are plentiful in Poland, particularly hazelnuts and walnuts. These are used ground, chopped, whole, blanched or roasted, and appear in the majority of cakes and pastries. Another popular ingredient is dried fruit, which is used for the more elaborate pastries normally served at Easter such as Layer Cake (*Przekładaniec,* page 171) and Easter Cake (*Mazurek Bakaliowy,* page 172).

The most important item in Polish baking is yeast. Self-raising flour, baking soda and baking powder are rarely used. Yeast lends the tanginess which is part of the recognisable flavour of Polish pastries. Fresh yeast, which can be bought from any health food shop, should have a creamy-beige colour and be firm in texture, but should crumble easily when broken up. It can be kept for up to a month in a refrigerator if stored in a loosely tied polythene bag. Dried yeast is more concentrated than the fresh equivalent, and one should allow $12^{1}/_{2}$ g ($^{1}/_{2}$ oz) of dried yeast to 25 g (1 oz) fresh yeast.

DOUGHNUTS
Pączki

Doughnuts are very popular in Poland and are traditionally eaten on Tlusty Czwartek, "Fat Thursday" which is the last Thursday before Ash Wednesday; at midnight on St Sylvester's Day (New Year's Eve) served with hot punch; and also at Epiphany (6 January), when a coin is normally hidden in one of them. At Blikle's – Warsaw's best confectionery – the doughnuts are made rather small and coated with chopped orange peel. They are absolutely the best doughnuts I have ever tasted. Unfortunately, although I tried hard, I was unable to prise their recipe from them and so the recipe below is for the more usual doughnut – which is *almost* as good.

Pącyki the Polish for doughnut, means bud, and it is easy to see why doughnuts are so named.

Makes approximately 16

....

> **900 g (2 lb) flour**
> **500 ml (scant 1 pint) water**
> **50 g (2 oz) dried yeast or 100 g (4 oz) fresh yeast**
> **250 ml (scant $^1/_2$ pint) sunflower oil**
> **salt**
> **flour for sprinkling**
> **oil for deep-frying**
> **caster sugar or icing sugar for dredging**

....

Mix half the flour with 250 ml (scant $^1/_2$ pint) of lukewarm water and the yeast. Leave to rise in a warm place for 20 minutes. When it begins to rise, mix in the remaining flour and water and the sunflower oil. Sprinkle a little salt on the dough and knead until it becomes a moist, coherent shape. Sprinkle lightly with flour and leave to rise and dry in a warm place for 30 minutes. Do not leave the dough to rise for too long or the dough-nuts will have holes in them and absorb too much fat. If, when you press the dough with a finger, it springs back immediately, it is ready to fry. When risen, pull off pieces of dough and shape doughnuts. Set aside.

Heat the oil in a deep pan or fat fryer until it is very hot, and drop the doughnuts into it. They will need to be fried in batches, allowing space for them to expand. Fry until nicely browned on all sides. When cooked they should feel light when pricked with a toothpick.

Drain on kitchen paper. Pile up the doughnuts in a bowl and dredge with a little sugar. Serve warm.

NOUGAT
Nugat

This looked extremely easy when I watched my uncle Stas Jabłonowski making it in his flat in Warsaw. When I returned home and tried it myself, however, it was not quite as effortless as I thought it would be. It *is* worth the hard work, though, being quite the best nougat I have ever had.

Makes approximately 1 kg (2 lb 3 oz)

500 g (1 lb 2 oz) caster sugar
500 g (1 lb 2 oz) honey
6 egg whites, stiffly beaten
100 g (3¹/₂ oz) walnuts or hazelnuts, chopped finely
3 x 24 cm (9¹/₂ in) cake wafers

Mix the sugar and honey in a large pan over a lowish heat until they are well melted and thoroughly blended. Bring to the boil, and when the honey starts to bubble spoon in the stiffly beaten egg whites, little by little. Keep stirring. When you can see the bottom of the pan as you stir, the nougat is probably ready. To test the mixture, which should be brown in colour and opaque, take a tiny bit of nougat on a spoon, run it under cold water and then roll it between your forefinger and thumb. If it makes a ball, it is ready. Pour in the nuts at this stage; they should be absorbed immediately.

Line a cake tin or flan dish with wafers, placing one on the bottom and breaking up another for the sides. Pour the nougat in, top with another wafer and weight it down with plates or a board. Leave in the refrigerator to harden for 4-5 hours.

MACAROON CAKE
Tort Makaronikowy

To roast the almonds, and hazelnuts, if using, place for several minutes under a hot grill until they are lightly browned. They can then be ground in a *clean* coffee grinder.

Serves 10-12

For the bottom half of the cake:
butter for greasing
5 egg whites
250 g (9 oz) caster sugar
250 g (9 oz) blanched almonds, roasted and ground

For the top half of the cake:
butter for greasing
5 egg whites
250 g (9 oz) caster sugar
250 g (9 oz) blanched hazelnuts, roasted and ground,
    or blanched ground walnuts

For the filling:
3 eggs
250 g (9 oz) caster sugar
400 g (14 oz) butter
40 g ($1^{1}/_{2}$ oz) cocoa

Butter two cake tins approximately 23 cm (9 in) in diameter. Preheat the oven to 180C/350F/Gas 4.

To make the bottom half of the cake, whisk the egg whites with the sugar. Stir in the ground almonds, and pour the mixture into one of the prepared tins.

To prepare the top half of the cake, whisk the egg whites with the sugar. Stir in the ground nuts, and pour the mixture into the remaining prepared tin.

Put both cake tins into the oven and bake for approximately 40 minutes, or until a knife inserted into the sponges comes out clean. Remove from the oven and leave to cool.

To make the filling, briefly beat the eggs with the sugar in a bowl suspended over boiling water, until well incorporated. Cream the butter. Mix the cocoa with a tiny amount of boiling water and mix all these together. Leave to cool.

Sandwich the cake halves together with the cooled filling and serve.

HAZELNUT CAKE
Tort z Laskowych Orzechów

Hazelnut trees grow in abundance in Poland, and children are often sent to collect the nuts, which they crack open by the bagful on the doorstep on their return home.

Serves 8

7 eggs
450 g (1 lb) caster sugar
450 g (1 lb) hazelnut kernels
dash of vanilla essence
1 tablespoon breadcrumbs
butter for greasing

Preheat the oven to 180C/350F/Gas 4. Beat the eggs and sugar together until white. Grind the hazelnuts finely and mix with the eggs, together with the vanilla and breadcrumbs. Grease a 23 cm (9 in) round tin and pour the mixture into it. Bake for 30 minutes.

Cool and split into two rounds. These can be sandwiched with whipped cream flavoured with vanilla, or covered with chocolate icing.

Nut Cake
Tort Orzechowy

Serves 10

....

For the sponge:
4 large eggs, separated
110 g (4 oz) caster sugar
110 g (4 oz) ground nuts (hazelnuts or walnuts)
3 tablespoons dried breadcrumbs
butter for greasing
dash of Drambuie

For the filling:
300 ml (1/2 pint) double cream
dash of Drambuie

....

Preheat the oven to 200C/400F/Gas 6. To make the sponge, beat the egg yolks with the sugar until thick and pale. Whip the egg whites until very stiff. Mix the nuts with 2 tablespoons of breadcrumbs. Fold the yolks alternately with the whites into the nut mixture, finishing with egg white.

Butter a 20 cm (8 in) cake tin and sprinkle lightly with the rest of the breadcrumbs, to prevent the cake sticking. Pour in the mixture and put in the oven, turning the temperature down to 180C/350F/Gas 4 immediately. Bake for 40-60 minutes. Turn out on a wire rack to cool. Cut the cake into two layers and sprinkle both portions with Drambuie. Let it soak in.

For the filling, whisk the double cream and Drambuie until stiff and spread over the bottom half of the cake. Sandwich the two halves together and serve.

CHOCOLATE CAKE
Tort Czekoladowy

Serves 8

150 ml (¹/₄ pint) milk
50 g (2 oz) cocoa
110 g (4 oz) butter
200 g (7 oz) caster sugar
5 eggs, separated
butter for greasing
300 ml (¹/₂ pint) double cream
dash of vanilla essence

Heat the milk to boiling point, pour it over the cocoa and leave to cool. Preheat the oven to 180C/350F/Gas 4.

Cream the butter and sugar until light and fluffy. Add the egg yolks and mix well, then mix in the milk and cocoa. Beat the egg whites until stiff and gently fold in. Pour into a greased cake tin about 20 cm (8 in) in diameter, and bake for 45 minutes.

Test the cake by inserting a skewer into the sponge: if it comes out clean it is cooked. If not, return it to the oven for a further 10 minutes. Remove from the oven and leave to cool on a wire rack. Divide the cake into two layers and sandwich them together with whipped cream, flavoured with a dash of vanilla.

Torte Aunt Jadzia
Tort Cioci Jadzi

This unusual cake is as decorative as it is delicious. Combining the rich flavour of cocoa with the tartness of damsons, the cake is also a contrast of textures. With its plain, smooth, biscuity base covered with meringue and topped with coarsely grated dough, it is a perfect accompaniment to coffee and is eaten in the morning or afternoon in cafés, and at home.

Serves 10

---

350 g (12 oz) plain flour
2 teaspoons baking powder
175 g (6 oz) caster sugar
2 tablespoons single cream
4 egg yolks
250 g (9 oz) butter
2 tablespoons cocoa
butter for greasing
1 tablespoon breadcrumbs
2 tablespoons damson jam
2 egg whites

In a large bowl mix the flour, baking powder, 2 tablespoons of the caster sugar, the cream and egg yolks. Melt the butter, pour it on and knead until the mixture is blended into a coherent dough. Divide the dough into three parts, making one slightly smaller than the other two. Mix one of the two larger pieces of dough with the cocoa and put both pieces into the freezer. Leave until frozen.

Preheat the oven to 180C/350F/Gas 4. Grease a 20 cm (8 in) cake tin and sprinkle with breadcrumbs in order to prevent the cake from sticking to the tin. Roll out the smaller third of the dough and press into the cake tin, smearing the top with the damson jam. Whisk the egg whites with the remaining sugar until very stiff. Grate the frozen cocoa dough over the jam, put the whisked egg whites on top and then grate the remaining plain dough over them. Bake for 1 hour 15 minutes.

PISCHINGER TORTE
Tort Pizingera

This Viennese cake was first called Pischinger after the name of the wafers used to make it. The name has stuck, and the cake has been widely accepted into Polish cuisine. It is quick and easy to make and provides a thin, rich, crunchy teatime snack with layers of wafers interspersed with chocolate.

Serves 10

> 50 g (2 oz) unsalted butter
> 175 g (6 oz) plain chocolate
> 1 level teaspoon caster sugar
> 50 g (2 oz) hazelnut kernels
> 1 egg yolk
> 4 round cake wafers

Cream the butter. Melt the chocolate and leave to cool, then stir it into the butter. Add the sugar. Roast the hazelnuts by spreading them on a shallow dish and placing under a hot grill, turning to ensure all sides are lightly browned. When roasted, grind them in a clean coffee grinder. Mix with the egg yolk, and add to the chocolate mixture.

Put one of the wafers on a round plate and spread a little of the chocolate mixture on it. Top with another wafer. Continue to make alternate layers like this, finishing with a wafer. Put something heavy on top of the cake to weigh it down and leave in a cool place for several hours. Cut into slices and serve.

CAKE WITH CONFITURE
Rolada z Konfitura

This was a favourite cake in Poland during the eighteenth century.

Serves 12

Mix 225 g (8 oz) of flour in a bowl with 225 g (8 oz) caster sugar, some water, 500 ml (scant 1 pint) warm melted butter and chopped lemon peel. Knead well and roll it out thinly. Spread on the dough some cinnamon, confiture or cream and roll up tightly. Seal the edges with burnt sugar and bake in the oven.

ROASTED ALMOND CAKE
Tort Migdałowy

Almonds are frequently eaten in Poland, in both sweet and savoury dishes, and used as a decoration. This cake is an excellent example of the rich nuttiness of roasted almonds, which have their own distinctive flavour.

Serves 8

For the sponge:
450 g (1 lb) blanched almonds
8 egg yolks
450 g (1 lb) caster sugar
10 egg whites
butter for greasing
$^{1}/_{2}$ level tablespoon icing sugar

For the filling:
50 g (2 oz) freshly ground coffee
75 ml (2$^{1}/_{2}$ fl oz) boiling water
2 egg yolks
50 g (2 oz) caster sugar
250 g (9 oz) butter

Preheat the oven to 180C/350F/Gas 4. To make the sponge, roast the almonds lightly under the grill and grind them finely. Mix the egg yolks with the sugar until they are pale and fluffy. Beat the egg whites until they stand in peaks. Mix all these together. Grease 3 cake tins about 20 cm (8 in) in diameter, and divide this mixture evenly between them. Bake for 45 minutes, testing to see if they are done by inserting a knife into the sponge; if it comes out clean they are ready.

To make the filling, pour the boiling water onto the coffee, stir well and leave to settle. Strain. Mix the egg yolks with half the sugar and add to the strained coffee. Set this mixture over a low heat for a few minutes, stirring all the time, until thick. Remove from the heat and leave to cool. Cream the butter with the remaining sugar and mix into the cooled coffee mixture.

Spread the filling over two of the sponge layers and sandwich them all together. Sprinkle with icing sugar and serve.

MACAROONS
Makaroniki

These little biscuits are a good accompaniment to morning coffee.

Serves 6

....

> **450 g (1 lb) blanched almonds**
> **4 egg whites**
> **450 g (1 lb) caster sugar**
> **butter (for greasing the tray)**
> **rice paper**

....

Roast the almonds lightly under the grill and grind them finely in a clean coffee grinder. Beat the egg whites until stiff and mix in the sugar and almonds. Heat the oven to 180C/350F/Gas 4. Grease a baking tray with a little butter. Place rice paper on it and drop small heaps of the mixture on to it, allowing a little space between each one. Bake for 30-40 minutes, until they are golden brown. Cool on a wire rack and tear off excess rice paper before serving.

JAM PUFFS
Dżemeówki z Ciasta Półfrancuskiego

Makes approximately 25

....

50 g (2 oz) fresh yeast or 25 g (1 oz) dried yeast
500 g (1 lb 2 oz) plain flour
15 g (¹/₂ oz) vanilla sugar
150 ml (¹/₄ pint) milk
250 g (9 oz) butter
2 eggs
jam for the filling

....

Crumble the yeast into the flour and add the vanilla sugar. Warm the milk, melt the butter in it and add 1 egg and 1 egg yolk. Stir thoroughly. Make a well in the centre of the flour and gradually add the milk mixture. When all is incorporated into a moist dough, knead well. Wrap the dough in clingfilm and leave in the refrigerator for 1 hour.

Preheat the oven to 180C/350F/Gas 4. Roll out the dough thinly and cut into triangles. Spoon a little jam into the middle of each, then fold up each triangle by turning the top corner down to meet the bottom edge and then bringing in the sides until the bottom corners meet to form square parcels. Pinch the edges together firmly, then brush all over with egg white, particularly round the edges to seal. Place in the oven for 20-30 minutes until lightly browned.

ORANGE MAZUREK
Mazurek Pomarańczowy

This popular cake consists of thin pastry topped with a sour-sweet layer of orange, lemon and almonds.

Serves 10-15

For the pastry:
225 g (8 oz) plain flour, plus extra for flouring
pinch of salt
175 g (6 oz) butter
175 g (6 oz) caster sugar
1 egg, beaten

For the topping:
1 orange
1/2 lemon
450 g (1 lb) caster sugar
4 tablespoons water
100 g (3 1/2 oz) chopped blanched almonds

Preheat the oven to 220C/425F/Gas 7. To make the pastry, sift the flour into a bowl and mix with the salt. Cube the butter and rub into the flour until the mixture resembles breadcrumbs. Mix in the sugar, then add the egg, incorporating thoroughly, so that all the ingredients are bound together. Turn the dough on to a lightly floured wooden board and knead for 5 minutes, until the dough is fairly pliable. Roll out to fit a 30 cm (12 in) flan dish. Butter the dish lightly and line with pastry. Prick the base several times with a fork, cover the bottom with greaseproof paper and pour on some baking beans. Bake blind for 15 minutes until the edges are browned. Remove from the oven, take out the paper and beans, and return to the oven until the middle is cooked and golden.

For the topping, liquidise or blend the orange and the half-lemon to a pulp (skin included but discarding the pips). Put into a saucepan together with the sugar and water. Cook, stirring from time to time until it becomes thick (about 40 minutes). Combine it with three-quarters of the almonds and leave to cool. Spread on the pastry base and sprinkle the remaining almonds on top.

PASTRY TWISTS
Chrust or *Faworki*

Chrust means brushwood, and this does describe the appearance of these sweet pastry twists rather well. They are otherwise called *faworki* which means little favours. When properly made they should be very thin and simply melt in the mouth. They are traditionally eaten on Ostatki, the last Tuesday before Lent, but are popular fare during Carnival time which runs from the 6th January, Epiphany, to Ash Wednesday.

Makes approximately 30

....

250 g (9 oz) plain flour
1 tablespoon icing sugar
25 g (1 oz) butter
1 egg
2 egg yolks
1 tablespoon sour cream
1 tablespoon vinegar or Polish Pure Spirit*
butter or oil for deep frying
icing sugar for dredging

....

Mix all but the last two of the above ingredients together in a large bowl to form a dough, and roll it out as thinly as possible. Cut into narrow strips approximately the length and width of a thin forefinger and make a slit down the middle of each one. Push one end through the slit and pull gently so that you have a twist in the middle. Do this to all of them. Heat enough butter or oil in a pan for deep frying, and fry the pastry twists until golden on both sides. Drain on kitchen paper. Pile on a plate and dredge with icing sugar.

*Bottles of Polish Pure Spirit are available at many off-licences and all Polish delicatessens.

Opposite: Polish Pancakes (*Naleśniki*)

JAPANESE TARTS
Ciastka po Japońsku

No one can tell me why these biscuits are called 'Japanese', but it is a Polish recipe.

Serves 4-5

....

For the pastry:
225 g (8 oz) plain flour
85 g (3 oz) butter
8 egg yolks
50 g (2 oz) caster sugar
dash of rum
grated rind of 1 lemon
flour for dusting
butter for greasing

For the filling:
110 g (4 oz) butter
110 g (4 oz) caster sugar
110 g (4 oz) ground almonds
dash of vanilla essence
dash of rum

....

Preheat the oven to 180C/350F/Gas 4. To make the pastry, sift the flour into a bowl. Make a well in the centre and rub in the butter, cut into cubes, and then the egg yolks, one by one. Work together thoroughly. Mix in the sugar, rum and lemon rind and knead briefly. Roll out thinly on a floured board and cut into rounds about 5 cm (2 in) in diameter. Arrange on a greased baking tray and bake for 10 minutes until golden brown.

For the filling, cream together the butter and sugar until smooth. Mix in the almonds, vanilla essence and rum to taste. Sandwich the biscuits together with this filling and serve.

Opposite: Poppy Seed Roll (*Makowiec*) and Cheesecake (*Sernik*)

RICH YEAST PASTRY
Ciasto Pół Francuskie

This is, of all pastries, the most used and loved in Poland. Little savoury parcels, sauerkraut pasties and sweet fruit puffs all use it. Hard to the touch and full of the flavour of yeast, it makes an excellent casing for any filling.

Makes 900 g (2 lb) dough

450 g (1 lb) plain flour
85 g (3 oz) fresh yeast or 40 g (1¹/₂ oz) dried yeast
250 ml (scant ¹/₂ pint) warm milk
1 teaspoon caster sugar
225 g (8 oz) butter
pinch of salt
1 egg, beaten

Mix one teaspoon of flour with the yeast, sugar and half the milk. Leave it in a warm place for 15-20 minutes. Meanwhile, sift the rest of the flour with the salt into a large bowl, cut the butter into small pieces and rub it in. When the yeast mixture has risen and is frothy, add it to the flour together with the rest of the milk. Mix it quickly with your hands into a coherent shape. Knead thoroughly, ensuring that the butter is well integrated; this doesn't take long. Wrap in clingfilm and leave in the refrigerator for 2 hours at least, or even overnight. It should have a brittle consistency.

Roll out the dough to the thickness you require and cut out the shapes you want. Fill with whatever you like, cover and seal the edges with beaten egg. Brush all over with the egg and bake in a preheated oven at 220C/425F/Gas 7 for 30-40 minutes.

JAMS AND PRESERVES

There are several varieties of jam in Poland, the usual sweet jams, the thicker, more concentrated preserves, and *powidła*. *Powidła* is a sour-tasting jam most commonly made from plums, although it can also be made from cherries, blackberries or gooseberries. All these jams are eaten on bread at teatime.

Polish jams form a large part of their export market and can be found over here in any supermarket, under the Krakus label. They are far more fruity than the majority of English jams and, being also quite a lot cheaper, make rather good buys.

QUINCE JAM
Konfitura z Pigwy

Makes about 2¹/₂ kg (5 lb)

> 1 kg (2¹/₄ lb) quinces
> 1 kg (2¹/₄ lb) cooking apples
> 150 ml (¹/₄ pint) water
> 1 kg (2¹/₄ lb) granulated sugar
> 4 oranges
> butter for frying

Wash the fruit. Peel, core and chop the quinces and apples. Put in a copper pan, pour on the water and cook gently to a pulp. Force the mixture through a sieve. Add the sugar and stir on a low heat until dissolved. Bring to the boil and boil rapidly until setting point is reached. This can be tested either by the use of a jam thermometer or by putting a teaspoon of jam on a cold saucer and when it cools pushing it gently, to see whether the skin that has formed crinkles. If it does, it has reached setting point. Remove from the heat.

Peel off the orange skins, removing as much pith as possible. Chop the skins into very small pieces, and fry them in a little butter until brown at the edges. Mix into the jam, spoon into warmed jars and seal.

Rose Petal Jam
Konfitura z Róży

This delicately flavoured jam is very Polish and is used, among other things, for filling doughnuts.

Makes 1 small jar

....

100 g (3¹/₂ oz) rose petals
200 g (7 oz) icing sugar
1 lemon
rose-water (optional)

....

Pick the petals of a full-blown rose. Cut the white parts off the petals (they are very bitter) and scald the rest with boiling water. Drain well and hold all the petals under cold water until they regain their colour. Shake free of water. Place the petals in a glass dish and cover with the sugar. Leave for 3-4 hours.

Put the petals and sugar into a pan and cook over a low heat, stirring frequently to avoid burning. When the petals are transparent, add the juice from the lemon – which brings out the colour of the rose – and continue to cook for a further 20 minutes on a low heat. If a stronger smell is required, a drop of rose-water could be added. Pack into a small jar and seal.

Plum Jam
(Powidła)

Makes about 1 kg (2¹/₄ lb)

....

1 kg (2¹/₄ lb) ripe plums
150-200 g (5-7 oz) granulated sugar

....

Use very ripe plums at the end of autumn. Halve and stone them. Without adding any water, cook slowly in a copper pan or preserving pan, stirring all the time. When the plums are cooked, push them through a sieve. Return to the cleaned and dried pan, adding the granulated sugar. Stir until dissolved. Boil quickly until setting point has been reached. Test this by putting a small amount of jam on a cold plate and leaving to cool. If the skin which has formed on the surface crinkles when pushed with a finger, setting point has been reached.

Pour the jam into clean warmed jars and seal tightly. The colour should be brownish-blue and the jam should not taste too sweet.

This can also be made with cherries, blackberries or gooseberries.

UNCLE JULEK'S BLACKBERRY PRESERVE
Konfitura Wuja Julka

This recipe may seem like a lot of work but the full flavour of this concentrated jam is brought out by the step-by-step cooking.

Makes about 1 kg (2¹/₄ lb)

1 kg (2¹/₄ lb) blackberries
800 g (1 lb 12 oz) preserving or granulated sugar
¹/₂ teaspoon vanilla sugar

Hull and wash the blackberries. Shake off excess water, put in a pan and mix with the sugar. Heat the fruit on a low flame, stirring frequently, and when it begins to boil lower the heat and simmer, stirring constantly, for 15 minutes until the fruit has become pulp. Remove from the heat, cover the pan and leave for 24 hours. Return the pan to the heat, removing any froth, and bring to the boil. Cook for 10 minutes, stirring all the time. Cover and leave for a further 24 hours. Return to the heat again, boil and add the vanilla sugar. While still warm, pour into clean, warm jars and seal at once.

EASTER

I spent my first Easter in Poland while working on this book, and it made a very great impression on me. I was fascinated by the endless preparations I saw, in people's houses, in the churches and even in the streets, where the shop windows were filled with flowers and decorated with beautifully painted eggs, and I remember the smells in Blikle's – the best bakery in Warsaw – as *mazurki*, cheesecakes, *babkis* and other Easter delicacies were laid out on the shelves.

As in any Catholic country, Easter is a big feast in Poland, and after six weeks of Lenten fasting people make the most of the celebration. The work for Easter starts weeks beforehand, when the table decorations are prepared. It is traditional to have a white sugar lamb as a centrepiece at the Easter feast. The lamb may last for some years but it has to stand on a bed of cress which must be sown anew each year. A piece of linen is smeared with clay and then put over an upturned bowl. The cress is sown on the clay and watered. After a few weeks, it will be beautifully green and make a handsome contrast to the white lamb. Then there are the eggs to decorate. Empty egg shells have intricate patterns drawn on them in hot wax, using the metal tag of a shoe lace. They are then dipped in dye and the wax is removed, leaving wonderful designs. These eggs, or *pisanki* as they are known, are used as table decorations.

In the churches a corner is given over to depicting a scene from the Easter story. Each church has different ideas, designs and ways of presenting the Crucifixion and Resurrection of Christ, but there is usually a collage centred around a tomb representing the one in which Christ was laid after the Crucifixion and from which the stone was rolled away after the Resurrection. It is a great Easter tradition to go and visit some of the tombs in the various churches and many people are to be seen praying in front of them.

On Saturday morning the food for the Easter meal is blessed. In earlier times the priest would visit the houses in his parish and bless the food which would be laid out on tables for him – whole sucking pigs, hams, coils of sausages and a rich variety of cakes. Nowadays, a basket of food containing just a slice of each item is taken to the church and placed on a prepared table. The church is full all day with people coming and going with their baskets. Every fifteen minutes or so the priest will come and sprinkle holy water over the food and bless it, praying that people always have enough to eat and thanking God for providing what is there. This food is called *Świecone* (blessed).

The Easter meal, which begins after the service of Resurrection, starts with the sharing of a hard-boiled egg. A piece is given to each member of the family and good wishes are exchanged. Hot *barszcz* is then served, followed by cold hams or *bigos*, sausages or turkey and then endless sweet cakes.

On Easter Monday another tradition prevails. It is called *Śmigus* which means 'pouring Monday'. It is customary on this day for people to sprinkle water on each other. This tradition comes, I believe, from the time many years ago when people were christened once a year, at Easter. This is still remembered in the Catholic Church when we renew our baptismal vows during the Easter service, but without any symbolic sprinkling of water. The Polish sense of mischief makes the most of the opportunity, and the light spring shower often turns into a heavy autumn downpour. There is a wonderful description of an Easter Monday in Poland in 1892, in *Recollections of a Royal Governess*:

Early, very early this morning I was disturbed by a terrific squealing under my window. In a moment a second squeal joined the first, both in shrill feminine voices, and in accompaniment to this uproar came a chorus of gruff masculine laughter. Hastily I arose, thrusting feet into my slippers and hurried to my window, which overlooks the street running behind the palace. Two maidens I saw shriekingly protesting, but quite ineffectually, against several young men who were dragging them along the street. I could not think what their object was, but by the laughter I saw it was some joke. The kicking, struggling mass resembled a football scrimmage at home, and I could see that the girls were making the fuss more from an idea of keeping up conventionalities than from any real fear of the lads. But my astonishment and also indignation was considerable when, arriving beside one of the large pumps which are placed at intervals along the older streets of Lemberg, the romp ended in a pail of water being emptied over both girls, who, with their faces red, their hair hanging in strings and tousled from their struggles, and their frocks clinging dripping to their figures, presented a disgusting spectacle. The moment the water found its way over them, the girls were permitted to escape, and they quickly disappeared.

I was very indignant at what I termed this outrage, when to my surprise what should I see but the girls returning, all dripping as they were, their hands full of brightly coloured eggs, which they good humouredly and impartially distributed among their tormentors. I was vastly astonished, and as at that moment my own maid appeared with my hot water, I demanded an explanation of this unseemly public performance of two wenches whom I shrewdly suspicioned belonged to the Palace kitchens. She replied in Polish, 'It's the sprinkling, Pani,' and when I asked what that might mean, she looked bewildered and said, 'A custom, Pani.'

When I met the Count and Countess this morning, I described with some heat the scene, and it seemed to me the Count's laughter was a display of questionable taste, at which I was surprised, as he is one of the most truly refined men I have ever met. However, I have always said that morals were more or less a question of geography, so I contented myself with a mental shrug and concluded that jokes were rather the same, but I could see plainly that the Count was intensely amused at my outraged sensibilities, and every time I caught his eye I saw a twinkle deep therein.

After mass we drove out to the Baroness Cecile's for lunch. I wore my black lace dress and a toque trimmed with red roses, and the Countess wore a beautiful mauve silk trimmed with exquisite lace, and her lovely pearls. We found rather a large party assembled and luncheon was a very elaborate affair. We had finished our dessert when suddenly Count Potocki seized his finger basin, and raising it high in the air, deliberately emptied the contents upon the Paris hat of the lady upon his right.

With that signal every man at the table caught upjugs and carafe and a wild turmoil ensued, the deluge sparing none. The table was a lake of running water. Exquisite creations of French millinery wilted and became masses of damp straw and muslin; toilettes from Vienna ran their wet colours into petticoats from Paris; powder disappeared and fringes hung in straight, unbecoming wisps; daintily silk stockinged feet sloshed in their soaked slippers, and I saw re-enacted the scene of this morning, with the difference that now the romp was between lords and ladies, in place of kitchen maids and soldiers.

For myself, I had taken refuge behind a tall palm, where presently I was discovered by a small gentleman who rushed wildly at me, carafe in hand. So enraged was I at the bare thought of such an indignity being perpetrated upon me, that I drew myself up to the full height of my five feet ten inches, glared ferociously at him, and exclaimed in my most tragic tones (it would have been a tragedy for me had my lace dress been spoiled), 'Ne Morgena, Ne Morgena!'

Poor little man! Never shall I forget his crestfallen expression. A moment before he had been the life of the mad party, his eyes dancing, his little feet scarcely touching the floor, so quickly was he dodging here, there and everywhere, douching this lady and then that, until at last he had met his Waterloo in me.

'But Mademoiselle, it is the sprinkling', he stammered.

'I decline to be sprinkled', I replied with withering scorn. At this point Count Badem appeared, roaring with laughter (I didn't think it was funny), and explained that I was a foreigner, unused to their customs – in fact, an Englishwoman, as though that would account for any mad eccentricity upon my part – and drew my gallantly inclined, but now thoroughly saddened, persecutor off, while I made my escape to the drawing room.

In a very short time our carriage was announced, the drenched ladies were wrapped well in rugs, tucked into their equipages, and we were driven swiftly home. The Badenis have been laughing at me all the evening, but I do not care for such silly nonsensical customs. It is bad enough in the stables, but I must say I think it is disgusting in the drawing room. I am told, however, that it is universal in this part of the world – a relic of the old days when each person carried a jar of Holy Water and sprinkled lightly his neighbours and friends. Next Easter Monday I shall stop at home!

EASTER MENU

A variety of dishes is commonly seen on the Easter table, but cakes predominate at this festival, and several are made exclusively at Easter time. Some examples of typical Easter fare are as follows:

Clear Beetroot Soup

Hunter's Stew

Cold Meats with Cumberland Sauce and Mayonnaise

Roast Turkey with Raisin Stuffing

Stuffed Sucking Pig

Layer Cake

Easter Cake

Cheesecake

Easter Yeast Cake

Paskha

Royal Cake

LENT WINE SOUP
Postna Zupa

This eighteenth century recipe makes a very warming start to any meal.

Take a small quantity of red wine and mix with a little flour until
smooth. Stir in more red wine – as much as is needed, depending
on the number of guests – and bring to the boil. Cook for some
time, Add sugar, cinnamon and saffron just before serving. Serve
with white bread.

LENTEN HERRINGS
Postne Śledzie

Traditionally the poor herring was eaten much during Lent, as meat was
forbidden throughout the whole forty days. On Good Friday revenge
would be taken and herrings would be hung on a branch for punishment
'that for six weeks it had ruled over meat, starving human stomachs with
its meagre nourishment'. Herring is actually much loved in Poland and
eaten widely as a first course before a more substantial meat dish, except
for fast days when herring alone is supposed to satisfy one's hunger. It is
normally served with sour cream and accompanied by onions or hard-
boiled eggs.

Serves 4

12 salted herring fillets
2 onions
10 black peppercorns
1 bay leaf, cut into pieces
5 slices of lemon, without pips or rind
300 ml (½ pint) sour cream

Arrange the herrings and seasonings in alternate layers in a glass
bowl or jar. Pour the sour cream over and leave for 24 hours to enable the
flavours to mingle.
Serve with baked potatoes.

BEETROOT SOUP
Barszcz

This classic beetroot soup is made with beef stock rather than the vegetable stock used for the meatless feast of Christmas.

Serves 8

....

2 litres (3¹/₂ pints) good beef stock

1 onion, peeled and chopped

1 bouquet garni

small handful dried mushrooms (presoaked in
  warm water for 30 minutes)

3 uncooked medium-sized beetroot, peeled and
  sliced thickly

300 ml (¹/₂ pint) kwas (see page 17)

1 teaspoon sugar

....

Heat the beef stock in a large pan. Add the onion, the bouquet garni, mushrooms and beetroot. Boil for about an hour. Strain the soup and stir the *kwas* into the clear hot liquid. Add sugar to taste and reheat, if necessary, without boiling.

HUNTER'S STEW
Bigos

Bigos is the national dish of Poland. Ancient in origin, it was made in a cauldron and cooked over a fire. The ingredients were whatever game from the forest the hunters had shot, along with sauerkraut and smoked meat which travelled so well. Mickiewicz's description in *Pan Tadeusz* of *bigos* being cooked conjures up the taste perfectly.

> They heap dry logs and heather in a pile;
> The fire spurts forth and like a grey pine tree
> Spreads out aloft a smoky canopy.
> Tripods are made above the flames with pikes
> And bellied cauldrons hung upon the spikes.
> They bring out vegetables, bread and stocks
> of meal and roasted meat ...
>
> The bigos is being cooked. No word can tell
> the wonder of its colour, taste and smell;
> mere words and rhymes are jingling sounds, whose sense
> no city stomach really comprehends ...
>
> But bigos e'en without such sauce is good,
> of vegetables curiously brewed.
> The basis of it is sliced sauerkraut,
> which as they say, just walks into the mouth;
> enclosed within a cauldron, its moist breast
> lies on the choicest meat in slices pressed.
> There it is parboiled 'till the heat draws out
> the living juices from the cauldron's spout
> and all the air is fragrant with the smell.

Today the variety of ingredients in *bigos* remains. Some have mushrooms and juniper berries; others contain apples, venison, lamb or beef. Below is a simple and delicious version which can either be followed to the letter or used as a starting point. *Bigos* should be cooked in an enamelled or cast-iron pot but never aluminium. Serve it with a glass of chilled vodka (Wyborowa or Żubrówka).

This is best made – as is all *bigos* – two or three days in advance and reheated slowly each day for one hour. This gives the flavours a full chance to mingle, as the ingredients are slowly broken down.

Serves 8-10

50 g (2 oz) butter
2 onions, peeled and chopped
1 x 936 g (2 lb) jar sauerkraut
800 g (1³/₄ lb) peeled tinned tomatoes
1 small white cabbage
300 ml (¹/₂ pint) strong beef stock
250 g (9 oz) smoked sausage
2 tablespoons golden syrup
5 or 6 pork ribs

Melt the butter in a large flameproof casserole dish and fry the onions until golden. Rinse the sauerkraut in cold water, drain thoroughly and mix with the onion. Add the tomatoes. Chop the cabbage very finely and mix in. Add the stock, stirring in well, and then the pork ribs. Cut the sausage into small slices and add with the golden syrup. Leave the pan on a low heat to cook for 1 hour. Remove from the heat and leave, covered, for 24 hours. Cook for a further hour the following day, and another hour the day before serving.

ROAST TURKEY WITH RAISIN STUFFING
Pieczony Indyk z Rodzynkami

Serves 8

4.5 kg (10 lb) dressed turkey with giblets
butter for cooking
4 slices bacon

For the stuffing:
125 g (4^1/$_2$ oz) stale white bread
a little warm milk for soaking
1 turkey liver
100 g (3^1/$_2$ oz) butter
2 eggs, separated
salt and pepper
4 tablespoons parsley
pinch of nutmeg
pinch of sugar
125 g (4^1/$_2$ oz) raisins
4 tablespoons breadcrumbs

To prepare the turkey for cooking, remove the giblets, put the liver to one side for use in the stuffing and keep the rest for making stock with the bones. Coat the bird with a little softened butter and lay the bacon slices over its breast. Preheat the oven to 200C/400F/Gas 6.

To make the stuffing, put the bread in a little warm milk and leave until soft. Remove and squeeze out excess liquid. Put the bread into a blender with the liver and mix to a smooth paste. Cream the butter and beat in the egg yolks. Pour into the blender, season with salt, pepper, parsley, nutmeg and sugar and mix again. Transfer to a bowl and stir in the raisins. Whisk the egg whites until stiff and fold in. Lastly, thoroughly incorporate the breadcrumbs.

Stuff the turkey and cover the bird with aluminium foil. Roast for 1 hour, then reduce the oven temperature to 180C/350F/Gas 4 for a further 2 hours, removing the foil and the bacon for the last hour to allow the bird to brown.

STUFFED SUCKING PIG
Prosie Nadziewane

Before the Second World War, this was traditional fare at Easter, and the sucking pig would make a wonderful centrepiece on the Easter table, along with the cold hams, sausages, and cakes. Nowadays it is eaten rarely, being so expensive. The stuffing, of which there are several varieties, is considered the most important element of the dish. Sucking pig can be bought to order at good butchers in Britain.

Serves 12-14

5.5 kg-6 kg (12-13$^1/_2$ lb) sucking pig, trussed and
    oven-ready, with giblets
300 ml ($^1/_2$ pint) beer
300 ml ($^1/_2$ pint) melted butter

For the stuffing:

1. LIVER STUFFING
(Farsz Podróbkowy)

600 ml (1 pint) water
lungs, liver and heart of the sucking pig
125 g (4$^1/_2$ oz) bacon
1 onion, peeled and finely chopped
50 g (2 oz) butter
2 eggs, separated
3 bread rolls, crusts removed and soaked in a little milk
$^1/_4$ level teaspoon dried marjoram
$^1/_4$ level teaspoon grated nutmeg

2. BUCKWHEAT STUFFING
(Farsz z Kazy Gryczanej)

600 ml (1 pint) buckwheat groats
1 egg
600 ml (1 pint) water
lungs, heart and liver of the sucking pig
50 g (2 oz) bacon
50 g (2 oz) lard or butter
1 teaspoon salt

^{1}/$_2$ teaspoon pepper
^{1}/$_2$ teaspoon grated nutmeg
pinch of dried marjoram

3. RAISIN AND ALMOND STUFFING
(Farsz z Rodzynków i Migdałów)

100 g (3^1/$_2$ oz) butter
lungs and liver of the sucking pig
3 bread rolls, crusts removed and soaked in a little milk
3 egg yolks
salt and pepper
1 teaspoon sugar
pinch of grated nutmeg
175 g (6 oz) raisins (scalded with boiling water)
125 g (4 oz) blanched almonds, chopped into strips
4 egg whites, stiffly beaten

....

Protect the ears and tail of the sucking pig with foil and put a wooden plug in its mouth. Preheat the oven to 170C/325F/Gas 3. Prepare one or other of the stuffings as follows:

Liver Stuffing
Boil the lungs and heart of the pig in the water, together with the bacon and onion, for approximately 20 minutes. Mince thoroughly. Cream the butter and stir in the egg yolks. Squeeze any excess liquid from the bread and add to the butter and eggs, mixing in thoroughly with your hands until you have a smooth mixture. Chop the raw liver finely and incorporate with the butter, eggs and bread. Next, mix in the lungs, heart, bacon and onion. Add the marjoram and nutmeg and work the whole mixture into a smooth paste. Whisk the egg whites until stiff and fold in. Stuff the sucking pig with this mixture.

Buckwheat Stuffing
Wash the buckwheat, crack the raw egg into it and toss well, making sure the egg coats all the grains. Leave to dry. Pour the water into a casserole dish and add the lungs, heart and bacon. Bring to the boil and simmer for 25 minutes. Remove the giblets and the bacon from the water, setting to one side. Bring the water back to the boil, stir in the buckwheat and boil for 5 minutes. Add the lard or butter, salt, pepper, nutmeg and marjoram. Mix well and leave to simmer, stirring occasionally until the buckwheat groats begin to thicken (about 10 minutes). Take off the heat and put the pan in the oven, turned up to 180C/350F/Gas 4, for 50-60 minutes. Remove from the oven, put the buckwheat into a bowl and leave

to cool. Mince the cooked giblets and liquidise the liver (or force it through a sieve). Mix all ingredients together and stuff the pig.

Raisin and Almond Stuffing

Melt 25 g (1 oz) butter in a small pan and add the liver and lungs to it, with a little water to prevent burning. Simmer until the meat is lightly browned. Squeeze the milk out of the bread rolls and mince with the giblets. Cream the remaining butter until light and fluffy, beating in the egg yolks. Mix with the bread and giblets. Season with salt to taste, sugar and a pinch of pepper and nutmeg. Mix thoroughly. Stir in the scalded raisins and blanched chopped almonds. Fold in the stiffly beaten egg whites and proceed to stuff the pig.

When the sucking pig has been stuffed, brush the skin with some of the beer and butter and place in the oven. Allowing 25 minutes per lb, leave to roast, basting every 15 minutes, first with beer and then with butter. The sugar in the beer gives the skin a beautiful golden-brown colour, and the butter crisps it deliciously. When cooked, remove from the oven. Place a coloured Easter egg in the mouth of the pig and serve with tartare sauce (see page 122).

LAYER CAKE
Przekładaniec

Serves 10

For the dough:
25 g (1 oz) fresh yeast or 12^1/$_2$ g (^{1}/$_2$ oz) dried yeast
175 ml (6 fl oz) warm milk
1 teaspoon sugar
350 g (12^1/$_2$ oz) plain flour
2 egg yolks
1 egg
100 g (3^1/$_2$ oz) caster sugar
125 g (4^1/$_2$ oz) softened butter
butter for greasing
flour for sprinkling

For the filling:
5 fresh or dried figs
10 dried apricots
50 g (2 oz) whole almonds (As an alternative, cherries,
    prunes, dates or any nuts can be used.)

To make the dough, mix the first 3 ingredients together with
100 g (3^1/$_2$ oz) flour and leave to rise in a warm place for 20 minutes. Whisk
the egg yolks, egg and sugar until white, and stir into the risen yeast
mixture. Sift the rest of the flour and stir in together with the softened
butter. Mix thoroughly until all is incorporated.

Preheat the oven to 180C/350F/Gas 4. Grease an oblong cake tin
measuring roughly 18 cm (7^1/$_2$ in) wide, 3 cm (1^1/$_2$ in) deep and 28 cm
(11 in) long, and sprinkle lightly with flour. Take a third of the dough and
spread it over the bottom of the cake tin. It should be one finger's width
deep. On top of this spread a layer of figs, apricots and almonds, halv-
ing or chopping them if necessary. Spread the filling in a decorative
pattern, perhaps in lines of the different ingredients. Top with dough to
the same depth as before. Make another layer of fruit and nuts with lines
going the opposite way to the layer below. Finish off with a third layer of
pastry dough.

Place in the oven for 60 minutes. Remove from the oven and leave
to cool. Cut into slices and serve.

EASTER CAKE
Mazurek Bakaliowy

It is thought that the Turks, with their love of sweet cakes, brought the *mazurek* to Poland. It is now an integral part of Polish cooking, with enough different kinds for each day of the year. Although typical Easter fare, it is also eaten at other times throughout the calendar. This is one of the more ornate *mazurki*. Absolutely delicious in taste, it combines fruit and nuts on a crisp layer of pastry and a topping similar to hardened meringue but in which are incorporated the added flavours of lemon juice, vanilla and almonds.

Serves 15

For the pastry:
250 g (9 oz) plain flour
15 g (¹/₂ oz) caster sugar
pinch of salt
125 g (4¹/₂ oz) butter
1 egg
butter for greasing

For the filling:
200 g (7 oz) apricot jam
500 g (1 lb 2 oz) dried fruit and nuts (dates, figs,
    sultanas, almonds, walnuts, candied orange peel,
    etc., chopped)

For the topping:
1 egg
1 egg yolk
70 g (2¹/₄ oz) caster sugar
juice of ¹/₂ lemon
dash of vanilla essence
70 g (2¹/₄ oz) unsalted butter, melted
50 g (2 oz) crushed, blanched almonds
25 g (1 oz) dried breadcrumbs

To decorate:
1 handful glacé cherries or candied orange peel

To make the pastry, sift the flour into a bowl and add the sugar and salt. Make a well in the centre and add the butter, cut into small cubes, and the egg. Incorporate thoroughly by rubbing with your fingertips, and then work into a ball by kneading. Wrap in clingfilm and chill in the refrigerator for 20 minutes.

Preheat the oven to 200C/400F/Gas 6. Grease an oblong baking tin about 18 cm (7¹/₂ in) wide, 3 cm (1¹/₂ in) deep and 28 cm (11 in) long. Roll out the pastry and line the base of the tin. Prick the dough with a fork several times, place greaseproof paper on top and fill with baking beans. Bake for 20 minutes, remove from the oven, take off the beans and greaseproof paper and return to the oven for 5-10 minutes until the pastry is firm to the touch and golden brown. Leave to cool.

Reduce the oven temperature to 180C/350F/Gas 4. Spread apricot jam on the cooled base and cover with a layer of dried fruit and nuts. Prepare the topping by beating the eggs and sugar together until pale and fluffy. Add the lemon juice, vanilla essence and melted butter. Mix well. Stir in the crushed almonds and breadcrumbs, mixing thoroughly, and pour over the cake. Bake for 30 minutes until the top is firm to the touch. Remove from the oven and decorate with glacé cherries or candied orange peel. Leave to cool and then cut into small portions, as this is rich and filling.

CHEESECAKE
Sernik

Serves 10

250 g (9 oz) butter
1 kg (2¹/₄ lb) curd cheese
6 eggs, separated
400 g (14 oz) caster sugar
110 g (4 oz) raisins
juice and rind of 1 lemon
40 g (1¹/₂ oz) potato flour
butter for greasing

Preheat the oven to 180C/350F/Gas 4. Cream the butter. Push the curd cheese through a sieve and mix in gradually with the softened butter. When smooth, add the egg yolks one by one and the sugar. Mix well. Stir in the raisins and the lemon juice and rind. Whisk the egg whites until very stiff and fold in. Add the potato flour.

Grease a cake tin approximately 23 cm (9 in) in diameter, and pour the mixture into it. Bake for 1 hour 15 minutes, or until the top is nicely browned. Remove from the oven and leave to cool.

EASTER YEAST CAKE OR DROWNING MAN
Baba Wielkanocna

This cake is sometimes known as 'drowning man' because of the preparation, which involves submerging the dough in water. The ending is happy, however, as the dough rises to the surface unaided. This cake makes an excellent accompaniment to coffee.

Serves 10

225 g (7 oz) plain flour
4 eggs
125 g (4¹/₂ oz) softened butter
110 g (4 oz) fresh yeast or 50 g (2 oz) dried yeast
100 g (3¹/₂ oz) caster sugar
200 g (7 oz) raisins
1 teaspoon orange rind chopped and fried
1 tablespoon rum
butter for greasing
25 g (1 oz) breadcrumbs

Preheat the oven to 180C/350F/Gas 4. Sift the flour into a large bowl, make a well in the centre and add the eggs. Mix thoroughly. Dice the butter and incorporate gradually. Crumble in the fresh yeast, or sprinkle in the dried yeast and mix very thoroughly. Knead until pliable, then shape into a round and press firmly into the bottom of a large bowl. Cover generously with cold water and leave until the dough rises to the surface of the water (approximately 10 minutes). Drain off the water and add the sugar, raisins, orange rind and rum to the dough. Knead well. Grease a large rectangular cake tin and sprinkle lightly with bread-crumbs. Put the dough in this, pressing it firmly into the corners. (Alternatively, the dough can be shaped into a tall, round form, in which case *it* should be smeared with butter and sprinkled with breadcrumbs.) Bake for 35-45 minutes until well risen and firm to the touch.

YEAST CAKE
Babka

Babka means grandmother, and this type of cake was probably so called because the tall fluted tin in which it is normally baked gives the cake the appearance of a woman's skirts. *Babkis* can be flavoured according to taste, but rum or saffron tend to be the favourites.

Traditionally, when a *babka* is being baked silence must prevail in the house. No doors should be slammed and the cook must not open the oven door to look at the cake before the appropriate time.

The quantities given below make an enormous cake, but I find this worth doing, as it lasts extremely well and is delicious toasted and spread with butter for tea.

Serves 12

1.1 kg (2 lb 8 oz) plain flour
450 ml (³/₄ pint) lukewarm milk
175 g (6 oz) fresh yeast or
   85 g (3 oz) dried yeast
rind of 1 small lemon, grated
2 teaspoons vodka
4 eggs
4 egg yolks
175 g (6 oz) granulated sugar
pinch of salt
175 g (6 oz) butter, melted
110 g (4 oz) raisins
25 g (1 oz) cut mixed citrus peel
butter for greasing

Sift 300 g (10¹/₂ oz) of the flour into a large bowl and add the milk. Mix in the yeast, cover with a clean cloth and leave in a warm place for an hour to let the dough rise. Put the lemon rind and vodka into a cup and leave to soak for an hour. Beat together the eggs and egg yolks, and stir in the lemon rind and vodka with the sugar. Mix thoroughly into the yeast mixture. Add the remaining flour, sifting it in, and a pinch of salt. Knead for 30 minutes to achieve a really light cake. Add the melted butter, the raisins and mix in the peel and knead thoroughly until the butter has been incorporated into the dough and it does not stick to your hands. The butter should be absorbed by the dough within 5 minutes, leaving a moist but not greasy mixture.

Place in a tall, fluted and well-buttered cake tin, cover with a cloth and leave in a warm place for a further 30 minutes or until the dough has risen to the top of the container. Meanwhile heat the oven to 200C/400F/Gas 6 and when ready put the cake in the oven for 1¹/₂ hours. Test to see if the cake is cooked by piercing it with a skewer: if it comes out clean, it is ready; if it is still a little moist, cook for a further 10 minutes.

ROYAL CAKE
Mazurek Królewski

Presumably this cake is called Royal because it was eaten by the various kings and queens of Poland. Certainly it is fit for a crowned head, being a delectable concoction of crisp nutty pastry and delicate almond flakes.

Serves 8

---

250 g (9 oz) butter
6 egg yolks
400 g (14 oz) ground almonds
250 g (9 oz) plain flour, plus extra for rolling
250 g (9 oz) caster sugar
butter for greasing
50 g (2 oz) almond flakes

To make the pastry, cream the butter thoroughly in a bowl, mix in the yolks one by one and add the ground almonds, making sure they are completely incorporated. Sift the flour into the bowl and mix well. Stir in the sugar.

Preheat the oven to 190C/375F/Gas 5. On a floured board, roll the dough out to form a circle approximately 20 cm (8 in) in diameter. Grease a suitable-sized cake tin or baking tray and place the dough in it. Decorate with almond flakes, placing them close together. Cook for about 30 minutes, until lightly browned and firm to the touch.

PASKHA 2
Pascha

Although this is a traditional Russian Easter cake, it is also popular in Poland. There are several variations (see also page 135) including a *paskha* cheesecake, topped with fruit and jelly, but this is the original version, a wonderfully rich combination of curd cheese, eggs, sugar, butter, cream, nuts, raisins and fruit peel. The traditional finished product should be tall, round, white and brightly decorated, and was originally made in a specially shaped wooden mould, but flowerpots are now used to achieve the right shape. it should be concentrated in texture – like a dense mousse – so it can hold its shape when unmoulded and, being extremely rich and filling, should not be eaten after a heavy meal. This recipe for authentic Easter *paskha* needs to be prepared the day before it is to be eaten.

Serves 8-10

1 kg (2¹/₂ lb) curd cheese
6 egg yolks
350 g (12¹/₂ oz) caster sugar
150 ml (¹/₄ pint) single cream
250 g (9 oz) butter
pinch of vanilla sugar
1 tablespoon mixed nuts, chopped
1 tablespoon raisins
1 tablespoon almonds, chopped
1 tablespoon cut mixed citrus peel, diced finely

To garnish:
2 tablespoons red glacé cherries

Loosen the cheese by forcing it through a sieve. In a glass bowl, whisk the egg yolks with the sugar until white. Stand the bowl over a pan of simmering water, whisking all the time, and gradually whisk in the cream. When, after a few minutes, the mixture is thick and soft, remove from the heat and stir in the cheese. Cream the butter, mix with the vanilla sugar and the remaining ingredients. Fold into the cheese mixture.

Line a flowerpot with muslin. Spoon the *paskha* into this, cover with muslin and weigh down the top for 24 hours in a cool place. Any excess liquid should drain from the hole in the flowerpot, and you will be left with a firm, dense cake. Garnish with cherries and serve.

CHRISTMAS

The festival of Christmas is celebrated in Poland on the evening of 24 December. Known as *Wigilia*, it is the most important culinary event of the year and at one time the dinner consisted of twelve courses representing the twelve apostles. Today it is more modestly celebrated, but the labyrinth of traditions remain.

The dinner is a meatless one, and even animal fats are not used in the preparation of the food. All the other elements of the land though, are present at the table: mushrooms from the woods, cereal from the fields, fish from the water and fruit from the orchard.

With dinner eaten, carols sung and presents distributed, the evening finishes with midnight mass. On Christmas Day itself lunch may well consist of a turkey, but by then the festivities of a Polish Christmas are really over.

Each family, from peasants to princes, has its private variations on Poland's Christmas tradition, and my aunt remembers her childhood Christmases during the 1920s and 1930s.

Born Countess Anna Wolańska, she was brought up at the great estate and ancient castle of Grzymałów. Grzymałów passed to my aunt's family in the 1830s. Once one of Poland's richest properties, in 1818 Grzymałów comprised some thirty-seven villages and three towns, its castle, park and folwark (home farm) being known as the *klucz Grzymałówski* or key of Grzymałów. Grzymałów passed to my husband's family in the 1830s and remained in their hands until the Russians invaded in 1939. In 1944 the Red Army bombarded the Germans in the ancient walls and towers and used the massive stones for road building. Aunt Anna's family survived the war, all save her father who disappeared into the depths of Russia's prisons and whose fate remains unknown.

> How well I remember those childhood years before the war, and the traditions unchanged by the generations and the growing excitement as our favourite day approached – *Wigilia*, Christmas Eve.
>
> The day began when my fur-clad father and several of our neighbours departed to Grzymałów's woods to hunt hare and foxes, occupying themselves with their sport until early afternoon while the household prepared for the day and we children, under the watchful eyes of our teachers, would ski on the gentle slopes of the castle's park.
>
> Red-faced, the hunters returned from the frost and snow and joined us for lunch. We would start with a caraway soup neither my sister nor brothers nor I really liked, though how virtuous we felt on such a religious day to suffer so! Our main course was sardines as well as herrings, but dressed in a mild sour cream sauce

rather than with the home-made vinegar, onions and spices eaten by the adults. With the grown-ups, however, we shared burnt fingers on the mounds of baked potatoes brought piping hot from the kitchens, together with a sweet-sour salad or ripe sauerkraut decanted from one of the two huge barrels in the pantry, which weeks before the maid had prepared in the golden days of autumn enough to last us the whole year!

Lunch over, Nurse Bońcia Hania put us children to bed, yet we minded little this winter siesta as time passed more quickly in the warm embrace of sleep, hastening on the advent of that first star which heralded the feasting and festivity. Prior to that enchanted time the household was quietly alive with the preparations, while later Father would tell us wonderful stories of shepherds in Bethlehem and the baby Jesus and the three wise men from faraway countries, all enriched with a tapestry of beautiful but invented detail.

At last, the star sighted, her twinkle's authenticity confirmed by Mother, we gathered at the beating of a Chinese gong to process gaily in our finery into the large dining room on the first floor. Sometimes, if the frost was exceptionally hard, we used a smaller dining room on the second floor but the table was always strewn with hay to, symbolize the manger and then covered with a snow-white cloth illuminated by candelabra and bedecked with wine glasses, which glinted in the candleglow as they wobbled on the uneven surface awaiting their inevitable spill. And over in the corner stood a tall wheatsheaf to assure a good harvest in the new year.

My parents were the first to enter and we children excitedly followed. Behind us, if I recall the protocol, came old Miss Olga Tebinko, mother's indulgent *dame de compagnie*, a wonderful pianist taught by Mikuli, Chopin's pupil. Next the threatening presence of Nurse Bońcia Hania followed by our two teachers, 'Lipenia' – Miss Janina Lipska – and the boyish Mr Kaczyński. Finally came the servants led by 'Nińcia' – the eccentric old Agnieszkza SzIagan who had been with the family since she was a young serving maid but now held the high dignity of castle *klucznica* or housekeeper. Behind strode the imposing figure of our cook, then Milka the kitchen maid, poor Marynia who suffered under Nurse Bońcia Hania's iron hand, the butler, the footman, the chauffeur, the coachman and lastly the gardener and undergardener. All processed in various states of humility or affected grandeur, to be received in the dining room by Mother and Father and offered the oplatek from a plateful of such wafers blessed by Grzymałów's priest, Canon Kruczkiewicz. Putting aside quarrels and household jealousies for once, they broke the *opłatek* with one another, wishing all good things for Christmas and in the forthcoming year.

The servants then departed to their big *Wigilia* downstairs, except for Nińcia and the footman who served in livery at table. Mother and Father at the heads presided over the meal, which commenced with the traditional clear red *barszcz* accompanied by dozens of tiny floating *uszka* which were like ravioli, each stuffed with diced mushrooms except one very special one in which Cook had hidden a nut!

Three different fish dishes then followed: carp Jewish style in a pale jelly; Mother's favourite, *krążki*, which were little rings of tench; but my favourite was pike served sautéed on two long dishes coated in a butter sauce thick with finely diced eggs. Accompanying these were puréed potatoes and all kinds of salads, with radishes and tomatoes from the greenhouse.

After, Nińcia and the footman served a russet-coloured compote of dried plums, figs, apricots and pears soaked in a syrup strengthened with honey vodka. Lastly came the traditional pudding of our south-eastern marchland, *kutia*, eaten only at *Wigilia*, a potion of poppy seeds, nuts, raisins and a type of large wheat grain stirred for hours in a mixture of cherry jam and honey. The grain was cooked but *kutia* was eaten cold and, according to the peasants, if a spoonful stuck to the ceiling a good harvest was assured in the forthcoming year!

The grown-ups washed the feast down with at least two sorts of wine, French or Hungarian, though we children, intoxicated on our own excitement, drank only water – goose wine, as Mother called it.

Towards the end of the meal Nińcia would inform Father that 'someone' had just arrived and urgently needed to speak to him. With mock irritation he departed and hurried to the drawing room which had been locked since the day before, out of bounds to all save my parents. There he lit the candles on the *drzewko* – our Christmas spruce. For years we believed the tree was brought just at that moment by the *aniołek* or little angel, who flew in through the window, though in central Poland St Mikolaj was responsible and in the west it was the *gwiazdor* whose name came from the metaphorical name for *Wigilia* meaning little star, *gwiazdka*.

All at table feverishly awaited Father's return, though once he took rather longer than usual and we waited impatiently, unaware of the blazing spruce my father and our guest, Aleksander Zaleski from the neighbouring estate of Ostapie, were desperately trying to extinguish!

At last he returned, and soon after we heard it – the urgent ringing of a bell by unseen hand! Aniolek had brought the tree! Now it would be there and even though we leapt from our chairs we never did see Aniotek flying fast away into the snow-filled darkness of the Christmas night.

Radiant faces gathered by the drawing room doors. Speechless, we gazed into that dark room flickering with the shadows of the tree's candlelight, searching her dense branches for the treasures she cradled there – toys, sweets, chocolates, spiced cakes, mandarins, figs and apples amid coloured chains and long-winged birds with strange plumage mother had once brought from Vienna. And atop this shimmering sight, almost touching the high ceiling, shone a huge silver star. Wide eyes slowly lowered their gaze and there on the old square table inlaid with ancient Polish coins from the days of the Commonwealth, lay mounds of presents.

Soon after, Cook and the servants came up from their *Wigilia* to see the tree and receive our presents, bringing layer cakes, tarts, coffee, tea and home-made brandies and vodkas of cherry, honey, sloe or dogwood. Before the happy throng departed, Mother struck up the carol '*W Dzień Bożego Narodzenia*', then the rousing '*Bóg się Rodzi*' and afterwards the soft haunting lullaby of '*Lulajże Jezuniu*' which once the homesick Chopin wrote into one of his scherzos.

I remember Mother's mezzosoprano and the resonant bass of Father and Cook, joined by a chorus of enthusiastic voices young and old from Christmas past. The chords come back to me now. I wonder, did one such happy refrain reach out across the song-filled night from Grzymałów's glowing windows and touch the little angel flying fast away, as now one reaches out to me across all the years and touches me so sweetly still?

CHRISTMAS EVE DINNER MENU

Almond Soup
or
Mushroom Soup
or
Clear Beetroot Soup with Little Ears

Pike, Jewish Style

Fried Carp
or
Carp in Polish Sauce
or
Carp in Jelly

Cabbage Parcels

Pierogi Filled with Sauerkraut and Mushrooms
or
Sauerkraut Braised with Mushrooms

Kutia
or
Noodles with Poppy Seeds

Christmas Eve Dried-Fruit Compote

Poppy Seed Roll

SOUPS

ALMOND SOUP
Zupa Migdałowa

Serves 6

175 g (6 oz) almonds
1¹/₂ litres (2¹/₂ pints) milk
110 g (4 oz) long-grain rice

Bring some water to the boil, place the almonds in it and simmer for a few minutes. Drain. Remove the skins of the almonds by pinching the nut between your thumb and forefinger. Pat the almonds dry, grind them finely and place in a saucepan. In a separate pan bring the milk to a boil and pour this over the almonds. Cook gently for 15 minutes. Boil the rice in another pan until just cooked. Drain, put in the soup tureen and pour the milk and almonds on top. Serve.

MUSHROOM SOUP
Zupa Grzybowa

Serves 6

100 g (3¹/₂ oz) dried mushrooms
2 leeks
2 onions, peeled
4 small carrots
few sprigs parsley
10 black peppercorns
1 tablespoon lemon juice

Rinse the mushrooms thoroughly in warm water until all the grit has been washed away and then leave to soak for a few hours. Pour the mushrooms and their soaking water into a saucepan and add 2 litres (3¹/₂ pints) of warm water. Cook, covered, over a low heat for about 20 minutes until softened. Wash and roughly chop the vegetables, add them to the mushrooms together with the parsley and pepper and simmer for 30 minutes. Strain the soup, reserving a few of the mushrooms, and add lemon juice to taste. Cut the mushrooms into thin strips and mix into the soup.

CLEAR BEETROOT SOUP
Barszcz

As this meal is a meatless one, vegetable stock rather than the normal beef stock is used as a basis for the soup. Tiny mushroom dumplings called *uszka*, or 'little ears', are the traditional accompaninient to this soup.

Serves 8

....

25 g (1 oz) dried mushrooms
1 celeriac, roughly chopped
1 carrot, roughly chopped
$^1/_2$ parsnip, roughly chopped
1 onion, peeled and roughly chopped
450 g (1 lb) uncooked beetroot, peeled and sliced
1 bay leaf
5 black peppercorns
750 mI (1$^1/_4$ pints) kwas (see page 185)
1 level teaspoon dill
1 level teaspoon parsley
1 tablespoon lemon juice
pinch of sugar
1 garlic clove, crushed (optional)

To serve:
1 quantity Little Ears (see page 186)

....

Wash the mushrooms and leave to soak in warm water, having cleaned them of all their grit. Drain, put in a pan and cover with fresh water. Bring to the boil and simmer for about 20 minutes until tender. Put the celeriac, carrot, parsnip, onion and beetroot in a pan, cover with water, add the bay leaf and peppercorns and cook for about 1-1½ hours until the beetroot has softened. Meanwhile, strain the mushroom stock, reserving the mushrooms for the 'little ear' dumplings, and set aside. Strain the stock from the vegetables and mix with the mushroom stock. Add the *kwas* and stir thoroughly. Chop the dill and parsley finely and sprinkle into the soup. Add the lemon juice, sugar and garlic if wanted. Heat the soup to boiling point, but do not allow to boil, remove from the heat and serve with 'little ears'.

KWAS

This deep-red beetroot ferment is the foundation for the classic Clear Beetroot Soup (see page 184), but is also used to sour other soups such as Polish Sour Rye Soup (see page 17).

....

450 g (1 lb) uncooked beetroot, peeled and sliced
1 litre (1³/₄ pints) water
1 crust rye bread

....

Put the beetroot into a large jar or bowl. Bring the water to the boil, remove from the heat and leave to cool. When it is lukewarm, pour it over the beetroot. Add the crust of rye bread. Cover with clingfilm or a piece of muslin and stand in a warm place (the bottom of an airing cupboard is ideal) for 5-6 days. Remove the foam from the surface and strain the clear beet juice into a suitable air-tight container. If kept in a cool place this will last for several months.

Once the *kwas* is added to a soup, the soup should not be boiled, otherwise this sour juice will lose its flavour and colour.

LITTLE EARS
Uszka

These tiny mushroom dumplings are the traditional accompaniment to
Clear Beetroot Soup (see page 184).

Makes approximately 20

For the dough:
75 g (2¹/₂ oz) flour
pinch of salt
1 egg yolk

For the filling:
**25 g (1 oz) mushrooms (reserved from the stock
made for the clear beetroot soup)**
1 onion, peeled
25 g (1 oz) butter
1 tablespoon dried breadcrumbs
1 egg white
sprig of parsley, finely chopped
salt and pepper

To make the dough, sift the flour and salt into a bowl and knead to
a smooth dough with the egg yolk and a few drops of water. Roll out the
mixture thinly and cut into small squares 5 cm x 5 cm (2 in x 2 in).

To make the filling, dice the mushrooms, chop the onion finely and
sauté both in the butter until the onions have softened. Mix in the
breadcrumbs, egg white and parsley, and season well.

Spoon a little of the mushroom filling on to each square. Fold the
dough over this to form a triangle, then join the two opposite corners
together, pinching the edges firmly together to seal. Bring a pan of salted
water to the boil and when bubbling briskly throw in the little ears. Boil for
5 minutes. They will rise to the surface when they are ready.

Drain the dumplings, put in a soup tureen or into individual soup
plates and pour the beetroot soup over.

PIKE AND CARP

Both large freshwater fish, pike and carp are the most popular fish in Polish cooking, and traditional fare at the Christmas feast. The carp, it is said by some, brings good luck, and I have heard that a scale from a carp, hidden in your wallet on Christmas Eve, is sure to bring money.

PIKE, JEWISH STYLE
Szczupak po Żydowsku

This is a good way of eating pike, as it dispenses with its numerous bones. It is a popular method of preparing carp as well as pike, and either would be suitable for the Christmas Eve dinner.

Serves 6

....

900 g (2 lb) pike, cleaned, with head

For the stock:
1 onion, peeled
1 carrot
1 celeriac
1 parsnip
1 cauliflower
salt and pepper
2 litres (3^1/$_2$ pints) water

4 large onions
2 tablespoons dried breadcrumbs
pinch of sugar
1 tablespoon grated horseradish
1 egg white
1 bay leaf
gelatine

....

Remove the head from the pike and reserve it, and cut the fish into six thick slices with a very sharp knife. Without piercing the portions of skin, take out the flesh of the fish and remove all the bones. Put the skin on one side. Chop the flesh finely.

To make the stock, bring the vegetables and water to the boil and simmer for 1 hour. Peel and chop 225 g (8 oz) of the onions, and mix to a smooth paste with the pike flesh, the breadcrumbs, sugar, horseradish and egg white. Stuff each portion of pike skin tightly with this mixture, securing with toothpicks. Arrange the packages in a fish kettle or other long pan so that they resemble the shape of the original fish. Add the fish head and pour the vegetable stock over.

Slice the remaining onions and add to the stock with the bay leaf. Cover the pan and simmer over a low heat for 1 hour. Remove from the heat and leave the fish in the pan to cool, then rearrange the portions in a deep dish so that the fish looks whole. Strain the stock, reserving enough liquid to cover the fish in its plate, but no more. Mix this stock with a little gelatine, allowing 11 g (0.4 oz) of gelatine to 600 ml (1 pint) of stock. Heat until dissolved and then pour over the fish. Refrigerate for 3-4 hours until the stock has set to a light jelly.

FRIED CARP
Karp Smażony

Serve this dish with grated horseradish and Sauerkraut Braised with Mushrooms (see page 193).

Serves 4

....

> 900 g (2 lb) carp, filleted and skinned
> flour for coating
> 1 egg, beaten
> breadcrumbs
> 110 g (4 oz) butter

....

Cut the carp fillets into small portions and toss gently in flour. Dip the floured carp into the egg and then press firmly into the breadcrumbs. Heat the butter until it is foaming, then add the carp. Fry until golden, adding more butter if necessary to prevent the fish burning.

CARP IN POLISH SAUCE
Karp w Szarym Sosi

This wonderfully flavoured sauce, rich and unusual with the additions of honeycake, almonds and sultanas, has a sweetness that goes extremely well with carp. Honeycake (available in small packets at all Polish delicatessens) is a moist, dense sponge made from honey, eggs and sugar and flavoured with ginger, cinnamon and cloves. Raisins and almonds are baked into it.

Serves 6

1.4-1.8 kg (3-4 lb) carp
salt

For the stock:
1 onion, peeled
1 carrot, scraped
1 teaspoon salt

110 g (4 oz) butter
50 g (2 oz) flour
50 g (2 oz) honeycake
25 g (1 oz) almonds, chopped finely
1 tablespoon vinegar
25 g (1 oz) sultanas
1 teaspoon sugar

Cut the carp into cutlets, wash them well and sprinkle lightly with salt. Leave for 30 minutes. To make the stock, put the onion, carrot and salt into 1 litre (1³/₄ pints) boiling water. Simmer for 30-40 minutes. Strain and pour into a fish kettle. Arrange the carp in this, and simmer gently – uncovered – for 20 minutes. Remove from the heat, drain the fish, reserving the stock, and keep warm.

Melt the butter, add the flour and cook gently over a low heat for a few minutes, stirring continuously. Slowly incorporate 300 ml (¹/₂ pint) of the fish stock. Grate the honeycake and stir into the sauce. Add the remaining ingredients and simmer for a further 10 minutes. Place the fish on a suitable serving platter, and pour the hot sauce over it.

CARP IN JELLY
Karp w Galarecie

This dish needs to be made a day in advance.

Serves 4

....

1.1 kg (2¹/₂ lb) carp, cleaned, with head
¹/₄ teaspoon salt
¹/₄ teaspoon sugar
2 onions, peeled
2 carrots
1 stick celery
1 bay leaf
1 teaspoon black peppercorns
juice of 1¹/₂ lemons

To garnish:
25 g (1 oz) blanched almonds
4 carrots, lightly cooked
2 eggs, hard-boiled

....

Cut the fish into 4 thick or 8 thin slices. Wash well, sprinkle with a little salt and sugar and leave for an hour.

Put the whole vegetables into a fish kettle together with the bay leaf and peppercorns. Add 1.25 litres (2 pints) water and bring to the boil. Put in the fish (the slices must lie side by side), plus head, and simmer uncovered for 20 minutes or so, until it is tender. Remove the fish slices, leaving the fish head and vegetables to simmer for another 40 minutes. This allows the stock to reduce and the gelatine contained in the head to be released. Mix in the lemon juice.

Pour a small amount (enough to cover the base of the dish) of the stock into a deep dish and leave to set firm. Decorate with whole or split almonds, carrot slices and rings of hard-boiled egg. Arrange the portions of carp on this and pour on some or all of the remaining liquid. Chill overnight but depending on the dish being used, until set. Turn out onto a plate and serve.

VEGETABLE DISHES

CABBAGE PARCELS
Gołąbki

Gołąbki, which means 'little pigeons', vary in their seasoning and stuffing from region to region. Sometimes rice and meat are used, sometimes rice and mushrooms, and sometimes potatoes, onions and a cereal. These can be made a day in advance and reheated when needed.

Serves 6

....

> 1 large cabbage, with big leaves (savoy is ideal)
> salt
> 175 g (6 oz) long-grain rice
> 2 large onions, peeled and chopped
> 450 g (1 lb) flat mushrooms
> 85 g (3 oz) butter, plus extra for greasing
> salt and pepper
> 1¹/₂ litres (3 pints) tomato juice, vegetable stock
>   or mushroom stock
> 25 g (1 oz) flour

....

Slice through the base of the cabbage and cook in lightly salted boiling water until tender. A quick way of doing this is to place the cabbage in a sieve, let it boil for a few minutes, remove it and peel off the first few layers of leaves which will be ready. Return to the boiling water and continue like this until you have all the leaves you need.

Boil the rice until just tender. Drain and reserve. Meanwhile, fry the onions in 50 g (2 oz) butter until softened. Dice the mushrooms and fry lightly with the onions. Mix with the rice and season well. Place a spoonful of the filling on each leaf and wrap it up carefully, folding the ends under like a parcel.

Heat the oven to 200C/400F/Gas 6. Grease a roasting tin and fill it with the cabbage parcels, packing them tightly together. Pour over enough tomato juice, vegetable stock or mushroom stock to cover them. Cover the tin with foil and bake in the oven for about 20 minutes. Remove the foil and replace the roasting tin in the oven for a further 10 minutes to brown the cabbage parcels lightly. Make a roux with the rest of the butter and the flour and add the roasting juices to make a gravy.

Any leftovers are delicious fried.

PIEROGI FILLED WITH SAUERKRAUT AND MUSHROOMS
Pierogi z Kiszoną Kapustą

Serves 8

For the dough:
300 g (10¹/₂ oz) plain flour
1 egg
salt

For the filling:
450 g (1 lb) sauerkraut
150 g (5 oz) butter
1 onion
110 g (4 oz) flat mushrooms

2 tablespoons dried breadcrumbs
sour cream to serve

To make the dough, sift the flour, add the egg, salt and sufficient warm water – 2-3 tablespoons – to make a loose dough, but one that holds its shape. Divide the dough into quarters and roll out thinly, covering the others with a cloth while working on one, to prevent them drying out. Cut out circles 7.5-8.5 cm (3-3¹/₂ in) in diameter.

To make the filling, chop the sauerkraut finely and sauté in 50 g (2 oz) of butter. Chop the onion and fry in 25 g (1 oz) of butter. Dice the mushrooms and fry in the remaining butter. Mix everything together.

Place a heaped tablespoon of the filling on each circle, fold over and press the edges firmly together to prevent them opening while cooking. They should be well filled. Bring some salted water to the boil and add the *pierogi*. When they rise to the surface, turn the heat down and simmer for 5 minutes. Drain, sprinkle the breadcrumbs over and serve with sour cream.

SAUERKRAUT BRAISED WITH MUSHROOMS
Kiszoną Kapustą z Grzybami

Serves 6

900 g (2 lb) sauerkraut
40 g (1¹/₂ oz) dried mushrooms
2 onions, peeled and chopped
50 g (2 oz)
lard
25 g (1 oz) flour
salt and black pepper

Rinse the sauerkraut in cold water. Rinse the mushrooms thoroughly in several changes of water and leave to soak in warm water for 1 hour. Chop the sauerkraut and put into a saucepan with 600 ml (1 pint) water. Bring to the boil, turn down the heat and simmer until tender for about 15 minutes. Boil the mushrooms in their soaking water until soft. Drain, reserving the water they were cooked in, and dice. Drain the sauerkraut and mix with the mushrooms and mushroom stock. Fry the onions in lard until golden, sprinkle the flour over them and mix in well. Add the sauerkraut mixture, stirring thoroughly, and allow to thicken slightly. Season and serve.

PUDDINGS AND CAKES

KUTIA

This traditional dish originated from days long gone when cereal stews were eaten and food was flavoured with poppy seeds and poppy oil and sweetened with honey. It is a custom that spoonfuls of this pudding are thrown at the ceiling, and if the mixture sticks it means the harvest will be a good one in the forthcoming year. Obviously the more honey in the *kutia*, the more likely it is to adhere to the ceiling!

Pearled wheat grains (which have the outer husks removed) are not easily available in this country so I use wholewheat grains, which are available from any health food shop. To remove the husks they must be soaked overnight, placed in a linen or muslin bag and gently beaten with a rolling pin, then rinsed in boiling water until all the husks have been washed away.

300 g (10^1/$_2$ oz) wholewheat grains, husks removed
250 g (9 oz) poppy seeds
400 g (14 oz) mild runny honey
150 g (5 oz) cherry jam
150 g (5 oz) walnuts
1 tablespoon raisins

On the evening of 23 December put the wheat into a pan and just cover with cold water. The following day, when the water has been absorbed, just cover again with cold water and bring to the boil. Simmer without stirring but making sure that it does not burn, until there is no water left and the wheat grains are tender but not boiled to a pulp. Leave to cool for about an hour.

Scald the poppy seeds: put them in a separate pot and just cover with boiling water, leave for 2 minutes and then drain. Repeat this process once more. Crush the poppy seeds in a coffee grinder or pestle and mortar, or put through a meat mincer 3 times.

Combine 90 per cent of the cooled wheat with the poppy seeds. Mix well and stir in 90 per cent of the honey. The colour should become blackish. Add the cherry jam, walnuts and raisins. Taste and adjust the quantities, if necessary adding the honey reserve to make it sweeter or the wheat reserve to decrease the sweetness. When the mixture is cool, it will be less sweet. The *kutia* should be served cool and taste very sweet.

NOODLES WITH POPPY SEEDS
Kluski z Makiem

Although this sounds rather unappetising, it is actually extremely good. It must be eaten piping hot. The best poppy seeds are blue-black in colour, and are easily bought in health food shops and supermarkets.

Serves 4

For the noodles:
225 g (8 oz) flour, plus extra for flouring
pinch of salt
1 egg

For the poppy-seed paste:
50 ml (2 fl oz) single cream
1/8 of a vanilla pod
150 g (5 oz) poppy seeds
50 g (2 oz) sugar
25g (1 oz) butter
rind of 1 medium orange
rind of 1 large lemon

pinch of salt
knob of butter

To make the noodles, sift the flour and salt into a large mixing bowl. Make a well in the middle and break the egg into it. Mix, adding enough lukewarm water to make a firm dough. Knead well on a wooden board until the dough no longer sticks to your fingers, roll it out as thinly as possible on a floured surface and leave it to stand for about 1 hour, to dry it.

In a saucepan, bring the cream to the boil, with the vanilla pod, and then remove from the heat and leave to stand, covered, to infuse for half an hour. Scald the poppy seeds as in the previous recipe, mince thoroughly and then crush in a pestle and mortar. Put into a saucepan with sugar and butter and stir well over a low heat until you have a thick paste. Add the orange and lemon rind, chopped finely.

Cut the dough into narrow strips and cook in plenty of fast-boiling salted water for 5 minutes. Drain well. Add butter and toss, ensuring that all the noodles are coated. Place in a serving dish and mix in the poppy-seed paste. Serve immediately.

CHRISTMAS EVE DRIED FRUIT COMPOTE
Kompot z Suszonych Owoców

This winter fruit salad not only tastes delicious but is also extremely pleasing to the eye, making the most artistic combination of bruised browns, russets and burnished golds.

Serves 12

....

375 g (13 oz) prunes
400 g (14 oz) dried apricots
250 g (9 oz) dried figs
250 g (9 oz) seedless raisins
110 g (4 oz) sugar
750 ml (1¹/₄ pints) water
rind of 1 orange or 1 lemon
3 tablespoons rum

....

Wash the fruit and cover with water. Leave to soak overnight. The next day, dissolve the sugar in the water over a low heat, stirring constantly. Bring to the boil and simmer for 10 minutes, uncovered. Grate the orange or lemon rind and add to the syrup, along with the fruit and the water in which it was soaked. Add more water if the fruit is not covered. Stir well and simmer until soft – probably about 15 minutes – then leave to cool. Stir in the rum and serve.

POPPY SEED ROLL
Makowiec

This is one of the most loved Polish cakes. It can be made with a soft sponge or, as below, with a sponge that hardens to a crust when baked. The moistness of the very tasty filling beautifully complements the crisp exterior.

Serves 12

....

For the roll:
50 g (2 oz) fresh yeast or 25 g (1 oz) dried yeast
3 tablespoons lukewarm single cream mixed
   with ¹/₂ tablespoon lemon juice
450 g (1 lb) plain or wholewheat flour
175 g (6 oz) butter

grated rind of ¹/₂ lemon
25 g (1 oz) caster sugar
2 eggs
2 egg yolks
pinch of salt

For the filling:
450 g (1 lb) poppy seeds
1 litre (1³/₄ pints) milk
175 g (6 oz) butter
225 ml (8 fl oz) honey
¹/₂ vanilla pod, finely ground
110 g (4 oz) ground almonds
175 g (6 oz) raisins
175 g (6 oz) chopped orange rind
3 eggs, separated
300 g (10¹/₂ oz) caster sugar
1 tablespoon rum or brandy
butter for greasing

To make the sponge roll, crumble the fresh yeast or sprinkle the dried yeast into the cream and lemon juice and stir to dissolve thoroughly. Mix with the flour and gradually work in the butter with your fingertips. Mix in the lemon rind, sugar, eggs and salt. Turn out on a floured marble or wooden board and knead thoroughly. The dough should be quite loose and not too shiny. Roll out thinly to a rectangle measuring about 20 x 30 cm (8 x 12 in) and leave, covered, while making the filling.

To make the filling, first scald the poppy seeds as described on page 194, pouring off the water when cool and repeating once. Bring the milk to the boil and pour it over them. Simmer over a very low heat for 30 minutes. Drain in a fine sieve and grind the poppy seeds until smooth in a coffee grinder or pestle and mortar. Melt the butter, add the honey, vanilla, almonds, raisins and orange rind. Stir in the poppy seeds and cook for 15 minutes, stirring constantly to avoid burning. Leave the mixture to cool.

Whisk the egg yolks with the sugar until pale and fluffy, and add to the cooled poppy seeds. Whisk the egg whites until stiff and mix in. Add the alcohol and spread the mixture over the sponge dough, leaving a good 2.5 cm (1 in) all round. Roll it up carefully and place in a loaf tin, well buttered or lined with buttered foil. The tin must be narrow and deep so that the dough can rise. Preheat the oven to 200C/400F/Gas 6. Leave the dough to rise for 1 hour in a warm place. Prick the dough with a thin pointed skewer to prevent cracking while it cooks. Cook in the centre of the oven for 45 minutes, or until the pastry is golden.

DRINKS

Poland is famous for its vodkas, and there is certainly enough variety to suit all tastes. Neat ice-cold bison-grass, rye or even pepper vodka make a wonderful preprandial drink and, to aid the digestion afterwards, there are numerous cherry, plum and other fruit liqueurs.

In the old days, however, beer and mead were the popular drinks, and were even indispensable to some. There is a story that Leszek Bialy (1186-1227), a prince from Cracow and Sandomierz, faced with the prospect of a pilgrimage to the Holy Land where beer and mead were not to be found, begged the Pope to release him from his oath to perform the pilgrimage as he could not survive without these drinks. He was released.

Beer was also the main ingredient in a cocktail called *Kaliszan* which was made with beer, french wine and lemon juice and then sweetened with sugar and sprinkled with breadcrumbs. The popularity of this concoction was due to the fact that it was known as a drink which cooled the throat and therefore allowed for further drinking.

Towards the end of the sixteenth century, spirits became more widely distilled and vodka came into its own. On the following pages you will find recipes for some. Others worth trying are:

Kminkówka	caraway-seed vodka
Śliwowica	prune vodka
Starka	rye vodka
Tarniówka	sloe vodka
Winiak	vodka matured in wine barrels for 5 years
Wiśniak	cherry liqueur
Złota Woda	gold-water vodka

Another vodka, which would have to be made as it cannot be bought, is *Żmijówka*. This semi-legendary potion is made by immersing an adder in vodka and leaving it to marinate for three months. Only for the brave, I imagine!

Some of the recipes in this section, in particular those where no syrup is added, may prove too strong, in which case they can be diluted by using any clear vodka. I would recommend for this purpose either Zytnia or Wyborowa, the latter of which is more generally available in England. These are 70° proof.

Polish Pure Spirit, which is 168° proof, is the spirit used in these recipes. It is available at any Polish delicatessen and various off-licences.

BLACKCURRANT VODKA
Smorodina

A decanter of this was given to us recently – more than that, the bearer of the gift, Jacizia Płodowska, had made it herself *and* brought it over from Poland for us. It certainly travelled very well and the life of this rich-flavoured vodka was very short once it reached our home. Jadzia makes truly wonderful vodkas and here below is her recipe for this rather unusual one.

Makes approximately 1 litre (1³/₄ pints)

....

> **1 kg (2¹/₄ lb) blackcurrants**
> **1 litre (1³/₄ pints) Polish Pure Spirit**
> **110 g (4 oz) caster sugar**
> **Wyborowa vodka to taste**

....

Put the blackcurrants into a large bottle, pour the spirit over them, seal and leave for one month. At the end of this time, strain the black-currants – reserving the spirit – return them to the bottle and sprinkle the sugar over them, turning well to ensure all the currants are coated. Seal the bottle and leave it until the sugar has dissolved (about one week). Strain the blackcurrants again, discarding them this time, and mix their liquid with the reserved spirit. Add Wyborowa vodka to taste.

Honey Vodka
Krupnik

This is often drunk on Christmas Eve.

Makes approximately 300 ml (¹/₂ pint)

....

> 150 ml (¹/₄ pint) honey
> 150 ml (¹/₄ pint) water
> 1 cinnamon stick
> 4-5 cloves
> tiny piece of nutmeg
> pinch of mace
> small piece of vanilla pod
> skin of 1 orange
> 300 ml (¹/₂ pint) Polish Pure Spirit

....

Pour the honey and water into the pan, bring to the boil and remove the froth. Put in the cinnamon, cloves, nutmeg, mace and vanilla, then cover and cook very slowly for 15 minutes. Add the orange skin. Now pour in the spirit, very carefully and slowly, and simmer for a few more minutes. Remove from the heat.

Strain the liquid while still warm, through either a very fine muslin or a filter paper. Bottle, cork and put into the cellar or other cool, dark place. After a week, when the sediment has settled, syphon off the clear liquid and pour into another container.

Krupnik should be drunk warm. A knob of butter can be added when it is being heated.

JULIUSZ KOMORNICKI'S
DOGWOOD VODKA
Dereniówka

I got this recipe from Juliusz Kormornicki who is mentioned at various stages in this book. For a long time he ran a brewery and so his knowledge of alcoholic concoctions is far-reaching. Dogwood berries are red cherry-like fruits which appear in autumn on the dogwood bush (*Cornus mas*). It is unusual, though not impossible, to find them growing wild, but they are a bonus in any garden, having pretty yellow flowers in spring and lovely autumn foliage.

Makes approximately 1.5 litres (2¹/₂ pints)

....

> **2 kg (4¹/₂ lb) dogwood berries with stones**
> **1 litre (1³/₄ pints) Polish Pure Spirit**
> **1 litre (scant 1 pint) Wyborowa vodka**
> **1 kg (2¹/₄ lb) caster sugar**

....

Put the dogwood berries into a large vessel which can be sealed. Mix the spirit with the vodka and pour it over the berries so that they are just covered. Seal the container and leave for 3 weeks. Strain the liquid, which will be red-brown and very sour, into another container. Sprinkle the sugar over the fruit and shake hard to ensure that all the berries are coated with sugar. Seal again and leave for 2-3 weeks. Add about a third of the sugar liquid to the waiting vodka and taste, adding a little more if required. It is now ready to be drunk, but will keep for many months, if stored in a cool place.

The fruit can be eaten, but is very alcoholic!

Gdansk Vodka
Wódka Gdańska

This multi-flavoured vodka has a potent taste, combining such strong ingredients as cinnamon, cloves, cardamon and juniper.

There is an old Polish proverb that goes like this: 'The best things in Poland are a liqueur from Gdańsk, gingerbread from Toruń, a maiden from Cracow and a shoe from Warsaw.'

Makes 20 litres (35 pints)

25 g (1 oz) cinnamon
7 g (¼ oz) mace
7 g (¼ oz) cloves
7 g (¼ oz) cardamom
7 g (¼ oz) anise
7 g (¼ oz) rosemary
pinch of fresh or dried lavender
a few juniper berries
25 g (1 oz) orange rind, cut very thinly
420 g (14¾ oz) lemon rind
10 litres (17½ pints) Polish Pure Spirit
10 litres (17½ pints) water
3 kg (6½ lb) caster sugar

Pound all the seasonings in a pestle and mortar and pour them into a big container. Mix the spirit with 8 litres (14 pints) of the water. Put the sugar into a pan with the remaining 2 litres (3½ pints) of water and stir over a low heat until dissolved. Bring to the boil and simmer for 10 minutes without covering. Mix with the spirit. Pour the liquid on to the spices, seal tightly and leave to stand for 2 weeks. Strain and pour into bottles. It can be used after 2 months, but is better if left longer, and if stored in a cool place will keep for several years.

Rowan Vodka
Jarzębiak

This vodka is especially good, and can be used as a medicine for stomach-ache.

Makes 2 litres (3¹/₂ pints)

....

> 500 ml (scant 1 pint) rowan berries
> 2 litres (3¹/₂ pints) Polish Pure Spirit
> Wyborowa vodka to taste

....

Collect rowan berries after they have been nipped in the first frost, or place in the deep freeze for 24 hours before using; the frost removes the sourness. Dry them out a little in a warm oven, but do not allow them to go hard. Put them into a glass jar with the spirit, seal and place in the sun for 2 weeks to infuse. Mix to taste with Wyborowa vodka. Pour into bottles and seal. This can be stored in a cool place for many months and is best drunk after about 6 months.

Plum Liqueur
Śliwkówka

Makes approximately 3 litres (5 pints)

....

> 2.3 kg (5 lb) ripe plums
> 3 litres (5 pints) Polish Pure Spirit
> 5 cloves
> 3 g (¹/₈ oz) vanilla pod
> 12 g (¹/₂ oz) cinnamon stick
> 1.5 kg (3 lb) caster sugar
> 750 ml (1¹/₄ pints) water

....

Crush the plums, with their stones, and put into a glass container. Add the spirit, cloves, vanilla and cinnamon. Cork and leave in a sunny place for 1 month. Strain through a piece of muslin.

Make a syrup by dissolving the sugar in the water over a low heat, and then boiling gently for 10 minutes. Leave to cool, and mix with the vodka. Return to the sunny spot and leave for a further 2 weeks. Strain again and pour into bottles. Cork. Leave in a cool place and drink after 3-6 months. It will keep for several years.

CHERRY LIQUEUR
Nalewka Wiśniowa

Makes 2 litres (3¹/₂ pints)

....

> 6 litres (10¹/₂ pints) black cherries
> 2 litres (3¹/₂ pints) Polish Pure Spirit
> 2 cloves
> 450 g (1 lb) caster sugar

....

Put the cherries into a large jar, reserving 50 g (2 oz), and pour the spirit over them. Crush the reserved cherries well, together with their stones, and add to the others. Drop in the cloves, seal the jar and leave for 4-5 weeks.

Strain the liquid into bottles – reserving the cherries – and cork. It should be left for 6 months.

Sprinkle caster sugar over the cherries until every one is coated, and leave for several weeks in a sealed container. If you prefer a more delicate drink, mix the resulting sugary liquid with the bottled liqueur. Otherwise, keep it separate and you will have two different varieties – in strength and sweetness – of cherry liqueur. Drink after 2-3 months.

CHERRY RATAFIA
Ratafia Wiśniowa

Makes approximately 4¹/₂ pints

....

> 4 litres (7 pints) ripe Morello cherries
> 2 litres (3¹/₂ pints) Polish Pure Spirit
> 7 g (¹/₄ oz) cinnamon
> a few cloves
> ¹/₄ vanilla pod
> 1 kg (2¹/₄ lb) caster sugar
> 500 ml (scant 1 pint) water

....

Crush the cherries and put them, together with their stones, into a large jar. Pour on the Polish Pure Spirit and add the cinnamon, cloves and vanilla. Seal and leave in a warm place for a month. Strain.

Make a syrup with the sugar and water. Stir until dissolved and then bring to the boil. Simmer for 10 minutes, uncovered, and then remove from the heat. Mix with the cherry liqueur and leave, sealed, for 5 days. Strain again and bottle. Drink after 2 months.

Kruszon Bevf

This is a very refreshing and not too alcoh'

Makes approximately 2 litres (3¹/₂ pi

2 oranges
250 g (9 oz) caster sugar
ice cubes
1.5 litres (2¹/₂ pints) light white wine
500 ml (scant 1 pint) soda water
lemon juice to taste

Peel the oranges and remove the pith. Cut into segments and place in a bowl. Sprinkle the sugar over them and leave for several hours in a cool place. Just before serving, put the ice into a jug or pitcher. Pour in the wine and the oranges, plus their juices, and mix well. Add the soda water, stir thoroughly and add lemon juice to taste if required. This can be made with apricots or any other aromatic fruit.

Mazagran

This summer drink is a most delicious and potent version of iced coffee.

To each cup of cold strong black coffee, add 1 ice cube, 1 tablespoon of granulated sugar and 1 small glass of cognac.

Cranberry Drink
Napój Żurawinowy

500 g (1 lb 2 oz) cranberries
1.5 litres (2¹/₂ pints) water
200 g (7 oz) caster sugar

Collect cranberries bitten by the first frost, or place the cranberries in the deep freeze for 24 hours to reduce their sourness. Wash and hull them, crush them well and pour the water over them. Crush them again in the water and then strain. Add more or less sugar to the liquid, according to taste, and serve cold.

OLISH DELICATESSENS

recipes in this book contain ingredients which can only be found at
icatessen specialising in or stocking Polish specialities. In Ealing and
ham in London where there are large Polish communities, these shops
ould be easy to find, but below I have given some addresses which may
be useful. (See also *Food Lovers' London* by Jenny Lindford, published by
Metro Publications.)

Enca Foods
2 Salisbury Pavement
Dawes Road
London SW6
Telephone: 0207-385 2462

Maryla (Polish Delicatessen)
1 Groundwell Road
Swindon
Telephone: 01793 521451

Mazovia Delicatessen
123 St George's Road
Glasgow 3
Telephone: 0141 332 4353

Parade Delicatessen Stores Ltd
8 Central Buildings
The Broadway
London W5
Telephone: 0208-567 9066

Prima Delicatessen
192 North End Road
London W 14
Telephone: 0207-385 2070

Wally's Delicatessen
42-44 Royal Arcade
The Hayes
Cardiff
Telephone: 029 20 229265

POLISH RESTAURANTS

There are quite a few Polish restaurants in London, some of which I have never been to, but here below are those I can recommend.

The Polish Air Force Club
14 Collingham Gardens
London SW5
Telephone: 0207-370 1229

The Polish Hearth Club
55 Princes Gate
Exhibition Road
London SW7
Telephone: 0207-589 4635

Wódka Restaurant
12 St Alban's Grove
London W8
Telephone: 0207-937 6513

INDEX